I0058158

MILLION DOLLAR-SALES CONVERSATIONS

Million-Dollar Sales Conversations
By Mike Klein

978-0-9905975-0-6 - ISBN Paperback
978-0-9905975-1-3 - ISBN Guidebook

Copyright © Mike Klein, 2013
All rights reserved.

Sales Edge Publishing

MILLION DOLLAR SALES CONVERSATIONS

THE FORMULA FOR CREATING LASTING RELATIONSHIP

MIKE KLEIN

CONTENTS

Overview 1

Sell Is a Four Letter Word, but Buy Is Not 6
We All Sell Something—Even You 8
What's in a Million-Dollar Conversation? An Overview of This Book 8

CHAPTER 1: The Million-Dollar Sales Conversation: Open Up Relationships before Trying to Make a Sale! 13

Successful Sales Start with Conversations That Lead to Relationships 14
Be a Giver First...16
You'll Never Stop Selling 21
Get In at the Beginning of the Sale—Not the End 23
Make Yourself the One Salesperson Customers Have Already Chosen 24
Practice Getting to Know Others...26
Sales Is More than Just Closing the Deal...................................29
Great Questions to Open Up a Conversation 31

CHAPTER 2: The Attitude of a Conversation 33

A Lesson about Attitude 35
Partner-Building Attitude 38
Be the following: 38
When to Say No 40
Expectations...41
Your Landscape of Relationships 42

All Relationships Are Unique—Personalize Them.................................43

Always Be Authentic 46

Develop Your Brand 49

Putting This Step into Action...50

CHAPTER 3: Seeing the Horizon of Possibility (Opportunity) — Now — Build Your Platform by Setting Goals 53

What Does it Take to Successfully Set Goals? 57

5 Reasons You Should Set Goals—and <u>Write Them Down!</u> 58

Figure Out Your Goals..62

Make Addressing Your Goals a Daily Habit 66

Stick to Your Goals: Stay Motivated and Believe...................................69

Let Nothing Stop You..71

How Adversity Can Help 72

Leveraging Your Goals and Goal Setting 73

Creating Your Roadmap 75

Putting This into Action 76

CHAPTER 4: Listening 81

Hearing Versus Listening – What's the Difference? 82

Two Ears but Just One Tongue 83

Why <u>Active</u> Listening is Important in Sales 84

What Active Listening Isn't...87

What Active Listening Is...90

Listen More, Talk Less 92

Listen Slowly..94

Listen Beyond Their Words..95

Breaking Down Common Barriers to Listening.......................................97

Practicing Active Listening...103

Putting This Into Action 103

CHAPTER 5: Encouragement..................................105

Why Encouragement is Important.....................................108
Encouraging Customers 109
Case Study—One of the Best Salespeople of All Time: Erica
vanderLinde Feidner...110
Show Customers Why They Should Buy from You................112
Encouraging Yourself 113
Encouragement: As Important as Bathing.........................114
Encouraging Your Sales Staff...117
Take Your Whole Sales Team with You into Success............119
Case Study—What Not to Do:
John H. Patterson of National Cash Register.....................121
Make it Look Easy to Fix Mistakes....................................122
Putting Encouragement into Action 124
For Customers 124
For yourself 125
For Your Sales Team..127

CHAPTER 6: Conversation Starters:
Small Talk for Big Opportunities 129

You're shy, introverted or not really a people person...........131
You don't understand various social styles.........................132
Start with a Noble Sales Purpose 134
Have a Story 139
How to Create a Strong Story 142
How to Craft Your Story...143
How to Tell a Story..144
Break the Ice and Establish Rapport.................................146
Determine if the Customer Will Buy..................................147
Challenge and Guide the Buyer..149
Putting Conversation Starters into Action 151

CHAPTER 7: Awaken and Expand Your Network 155

How Networks are Different Today 157

Face-to-Face Networking 159

Online Networking 164

For Someone You Know 165

For Someone You DON'T KNOW... 166

Grow Your Influence through Online Groups 168

Making Connections through Groups 170

Be a People Person... 172

Putting this into Action.. 173

CHAPTER 8: Action Steps to Take Conversations to the Next Level............................ 177

The Domino Effect 178

Step 1: A is for Attitude... 178

Step 2: Set Goals and Stick to Them... 179

Step 3: Listen Actively 180

Step 4: Be an Encourager 181

Step 5: Make Successful Small Talk for Continued Success.................. 182

Step 6: Stretch Your Network 183

Get to Work!.. 183

OVERVIEW

The cloudy March sky reflected how project sales had been going lately. Call it overcast and getting darker with a forecast of more lost sales to come. Both the weather and my day were looking foreboding, and I was feeling increasingly unsettled and anxious. It's not that I had a bad team. In fact, my team was one of the best I'd ever known. It actually couldn't get much better. I was working with a project management group on a multi-million dollar sales opportunity. The team included more than 10 people from several areas of our business: engineering, delivery, manufacturing, shipping, purchasing, and training. They were good, really good. We had been working on this opportunity for several months and we were almost done putting the final proposal together, but something still didn't feel right. Call it intuition, but I was worried that we had missed something.

Right before applying the finishing touches, I asked each team member how he or she felt about our relationship with the customer. They said things, such as "They like us," They have bought from us in the past," and "We did all the work; they have to go with us." Over the years, I've heard these same answers on hundreds, even thousands of opportunities, and yet we'd lost many of those opportunities.

Does this sound familiar? Have you ever lost a sale? Have you ever said to yourself, "I did all the work. I gave them the best price. I have a good relationship with the contacts I deal with, so they have to buy from me." Something clicked as I listened to their answers. I decided to keep pressing the group because this was a very large opportunity, and I didn't want to let this sale slip through our fingers. I wanted to be certain that we were going to win this one, so I changed the questions.

I started to ask them about the contacts we were dealing with and how well they knew them. They all sat up in their chairs, tilted their heads, and then looked at one another and back at me.

Tom, one of the project leads, said, "Mike, we know everyone in every department of this company. We know every step and issue they have in the supply chain: who answers the phone, who signs the contracts, and who is most likely to approve or disapprove the contract. We even know what brand of coffee they keep in the break room and who all of their vendors are. We know them."

I smiled at him and said, "Good job, Tom. We do know their company and their roles and responsibilities, but do we really know them as employees and, more importantly, as people? Do we know if the contacts we're dealing with have any kids? Do we know their favorite hobbies? Do we know what they like doing when they aren't at work? Do we know the last place they went on vacation? I think you get the point."

Tom nodded and looked around the group. I could see the "aha" moment on their faces. We didn't have those answers for any of the contacts we were working with, and we knew it.

I knew when I saw their faces that we didn't have the kind of relationships we needed. They recognized it too. We hadn't spent enough time getting to know them as people outside of work. That meant we were at risk of losing this deal. If we had pushed forward with the final proposal at this point, we would have lost the contract.

Obviously, the members of my team had spent a significant amount of time putting the right solution together; adding value and driving the price down. However, they had failed to cultivate personal relationships with the contacts.

Doing business with people is more than just doing business. In order to be successful, you need to build trust and add value. You do this best by building personal relationships with your contacts or potential customers. Never underestimate the power and influence of personal relationships in the business world.

People, not businesses, make decisions. A relationship is much more than just knowing someone's name. You need to know, respect, and genuinely engage with the people you are dealing with on an honest, personal level.

You've most likely heard the saying, "People do business with people they like." People can't like you if you don't know them. You have probably figured out what my team needed to do next, and it wasn't anything related to the final proposal. Believe me, the last thing the group wanted to do was talk about sales. But the funny thing is, we weren't talking about sales. We were talking about relationships. I knew we had a real need to understand how we were evaluating and looking at relationships with our customers and potential customers.

Relationships are a critical part of sales strategies. We had spun our wheels so many times before on projects only to lose them in the end. It was discouraging. Looking back at how we had done things, I could see where we'd lost sales—and it wasn't in the solutions area; it was in the way we approached and interacted with people. I think salespeople often overestimate how strong their relationships are with their contacts. That's why they get disappointed when they lose deals. They think they've put their best into a deal. In reality, they've just left out the linchpin that secures the deal—the trust people have when they have built a personal relationship with their contacts.

When you start to understand the dynamics of people and what they want, mastering what I call the million-dollar sales conversation becomes easy. Remember that people not only *want* to have relationships but also *need* to have them in business. In this instance, my team had a great opportunity the next day to start practicing building relationships and using some of the techniques that we had discussed.

Here, each one had an assignment to start building personal relationships. We discussed how to do this in various ways. One of the suggestions was to take the contacts out to lunch to discuss the final solution since they were expecting the proposal. It would be a good way to start getting to know them on a personal level and the easiest way to get in front of them one more time.

The team members put a powerful rule in place for the lunch: they could only ask *personal questions* of the contacts. No one on our side could ask a business-related question. Business-related questions could only come from the contacts. Interestingly, the team members had such a fun time with the contacts that they forgot this was a business meeting. The team was laughing, sharing stories about kids and family, and connecting on a personal level. Several of the people on the team even made plans with the contacts to get together with their kids who played baseball. The team realized at this point what real relationships are about. Needless to say, the team ended up winning the deal and built a relationship with this customer that, over time, turned into several million dollars worth of business. Around this time, the economy had taken a downturn, and we needed everyone to know that closing ratios had to improve. We also needed everyone to understand that when we open up a conversation with someone, we are selling, even if we don't mention our product or company. Our jobs were on the line, so every opportunity to start great conversations became even more important to us. I gave them the best advice I could: "Have conversations with individuals, and connect with each of them on a personal level." Develop a positive attitude and truly think about helping the person you're talking with. Don't think about selling any products. Instead, go with an attitude that *opening great conversations will lead to meaningful relationships, which could turn into million-dollar opportunities.*

I'll never forget the energy shift in the room. You could feel the tension evaporate. These newly created sales people got it. They were at the doorstep of creating million-dollar sales conversations. And me? I was on my way to a whole different experience in sales.

These were very successful strategies because they were always about connecting with people first. Further, these strategies focused on understanding the people we were dealing with, along with their wants and needs. These elements are critical to the success of any sale. Ultimately, opening up relationships is *always* about opening up a powerful conversation, which I refer to as a million-dollar sales conversation.

We have conversations every day. What I am referring to are conversations that are rich with meaning, caring, and connection. They require an understanding of what makes great conversations. What I will share with you in this book is a successful process to help you consistently achieve your sales goals. I've spent the last 31 years developing a process that works for me consistently, and has worked for hundreds of others. So far I've trained over 750 account managers who've collectively produced more than $1.7 billion in sales. Now, I'd like to help you become as successful as my teams and I have been.

Sell Is a Four Letter Word, but Buy Is Not

No matter what industry you work in, you've probably seen some people rise to the top very quickly. They have some sort of charisma that draws people to them. So what do they have that you don't? Absolutely nothing. It's simply that they have mastered the art of the million-dollar sales conversation. The idea of a million-dollar sales conversation means different things to different people. The goal may not be a million-dollar sale, but it might be something that represents what you view as the ultimate prize. It could be a first order, a new contact, a referral, or a meeting with a top executive. It could be a chance to lead a project. It could be a chance to interview for a new job or to accept one.

If you don't consider yourself to be a salesperson, the thought of trying to sell something probably sends shivers down your spine. Most of us have been hassled by a salesperson that just wanted us to buy something, anything, and when a salesperson is especially persistent and annoying, the entire encounter isn't a good experience. In fact, we may even decide to go to a competitor because of the bad feelings we get from a pushy salesperson. Bad salespeople create these feelings in us because we intuitively know their intent is to sell us something, and we resent it. We feel used and manipulated. We know the person doesn't really care about our interests. There is very little sincerity, and often even a condescending tone or a feeling that the salesperson has scripted the entire conversation. This is where the negative connotations of the used-car salesmen come in. We see these people as only caring about themselves.

Perhaps they don't remember your name or don't listen to what your needs are, or they don't ask any personal questions to form a personal connection with you. Any person whose overriding priority is to make a sale doesn't have your best interests in mind.

Successful sales people don't follow this mentality. When you meet them, there is a magic about them. They're working *for* you or *with* you, not *on* you. They approach you with the mentality that they can do something to help you instead of wanting you to do something for them.

You may know someone like this. The person was so helpful, and you had so much in common with him or her that you became friends. But what seems like magic really isn't magic at all. It's a whole new way to look at selling.

We All Sell Something—Even You

This book is for anyone who sells, and that includes you, even if you're not in what's technically considered to be a sales job. We all sell something. We sell ourselves during job interviews, business meetings, dinner dates, school, block parties, and so forth. Teachers have to "sell" students by motivating them to study. Politicians need to sell their proposed bills. You have to sell yourself every time you interact with people. If you're not interesting or expressing interest in others, no one wants to be around you.

What's in a Million-Dollar Conversation? An Overview of This Book

In this book, I'll provide you with a process for building great opportunities through million-dollar sales conversations. I'll begin in chapter 1 with the landscape of sales conversations. I'll share many actual stories to help illustrate the various conversations you can develop.

In chapter 2, we'll explore the many elements around what I call the *attitude of selling*. I'll tell you how to get into the right frame of mind when it comes to selling, and I'll share details regarding how to shift from a selling approach to a helping approach to create more value in your conversations.

In the book, *Give and Take: A Revolutionary Approach to Success*, Wharton professor Adam Grant explains how important it is not to come across like a "taker in a giver's clothes." Going into a relationship with an attitude that's "self-promoting, self-absorbed, and self-important" is a red flag—one that you can't throw up if you want to have a million-dollar conversation. Grant says that another red flag is the way you treat people. Your reputation always precedes you, so if you have a habit of "kissing up and kicking down," then others will know this and steer clear.

He also goes into other research that shows the additional benefits of being a giver rather than a taker. He notes that while you may start off behind other people if you're a giver, in the long term, you'll end up ahead of them. It only takes a small stone thrown into a pond to create powerful ripples that spread all the way across the surface. If you're truly a giver, you'll be someone people want to connect with, and you'll be someone they trust. The examples I provide in this chapter will help you to develop a winning attitude.

In chapter 3, I'll show you how to create goals for your near-term and long-term conversations that will help you achieve better sales success. You'll see how every one of your goals will serve as a major milestone on your journey.

Determining your goals, however, is just the start. You also have to look at the potential best-case scenarios for your clients. Once you understand what people are most passionate about, you can help them turn their dreams into reality.

In chapter 4, I share how to use your listening skills to start and develop million-dollar conversations. In order to truly get to know someone, you must develop the skill of active listening. When someone talks, you should not only listen to the words coming out of his or her mouth, but also listen with a mindset or attitude of ways you can use your knowledge and resources to genuinely help the person. For example, I had the opportunity to talk with a local pizza parlor owner at a place I had discovered several blocks from my dorm. As the business was located four blocks from campus, it was not known well by others who went to my college simply because they were unaware of it. I had worked at a pizza place in high school, so I knew a thing or two about the business. Pizza is an inexpensive comfort food, and most people want to have it delivered, especially college kids without transportation.

After listening to the owner complain about the scarcity of customers in his pizza parlor, I suggested he consider delivering pizza to the campus. I also suggested he stay open past eight, which is actually the time most students start craving pizza. Then I offered to deliver pizza for him in the evenings, as long as I got reimbursed for my gas and I got to keep the tips. The owner loved the idea. My suggestion worked out very well because in order to get a parking pass on campus, I needed to prove I had a job. As a result of our mutually beneficial partnership, his pizza business really took off. I also pitched the idea of giving away free T-shirts with the purchase of each large pizza. As a result, they got plenty of free advertising. The job served as a great way for me to make a few extra bucks, meet kids on campus, keep my car, and help the local pizza place build its business. By the time I graduated, the owner had opened up two more pizza places in college areas.

But how can you take your conversations to the next level to create opportunities better and faster? In chapter 5, I talk about encouragement. Everyone can get discouraged when they're trying to achieve their goals. Therefore, honing your encouragement skills will enable you to provide your contacts, prospects and customers with ideas and solutions that help them exceed their goals. It's not enough to just say, "Hang in there." Offering true encouragement is an art form and I'll show you how to develop this skillset.

Next, in chapter 6, I give you some conversation starters. Even if you're an introvert or "not very good with people," "small talk" is a skill you can master. In fact, small talk can lead to big opportunities. It's called small talk because you're basically just trying to find something small to talk about with a complete stranger. Million-dollar conversations start out with small talk and your conversations are no different. From there, you can take your small talk to the next level.

In chapter 7, I discuss how you can awaken and expand your network. Everyone has a network, but you need to analyze it to separate out the givers from the takers. You can then leverage your givers into sustainable *exchangers*. Exchangers are people who have taken the extra steps to keep your conversations going, creating new opportunities for both of you regularly. Connecting with them will yield both financial and emotional returns again and again. I'll show, first, how to become and an exchanger and then how to find other exchangers. I'll also show you why you only need a few of these terrific conversationalists in your network to get great results.

Finally, in chapter 8, I will finish with a series of additional tips for each step in the process of creating million-dollar sales conversations. Having a takeaway that provides all the steps of a suggested process in one place with additional tips can be very helpful.

Are you ready to begin? Let's get started.

CHAPTER 1

The Million-Dollar Sales Conversation: Open Up Relationships before Trying to Make a Sale!

After digging deep into his calendar and truly examining everything he did all day, Daniel Pink, bestselling author of *To Sell is Human: The Surprising Truth About Moving Others,* discovered that he sells something to someone all the time, and he believes that others aren't that different. As he says in his book, "All of you are likely spending more time than you realize selling in a broader sense—pitching colleagues, persuading funders, cajoling kids. Like it or not, we're all in sales now."

Prior to writing his book, Pink had reservations about selling, just as many of us do. In his book, however, he shows us that selling can be a different experience—that it can be good and even fun. But as he notes, the traditional ways of viewing selling are simply outdated. He says that, "most of what we think we understand about selling is constructed atop a foundation of assumptions that has crumbled."

Until we realize just how outdated traditional views of selling are, finding yourself in the middle of that million-dollar conversation is going to be difficult. So how do we get into such a conversation? How do we land that major deal? How do we get people engaged with us and move them to want to be engaged at the highest level? Having million-dollar conversations and getting people to invest large amounts of time and money on what we are selling is a process, and it can be learned and mastered!

First, you've got to figure out exactly what you're selling—and that something is you! Don't get confused. You need to spend time knowing the products you represent and the value they bring to the customer. However, salespeople sometimes forget that selling is about connecting with people and building trust. It is critical that you understand how to solve your customer's needs and sell yourself. The great thing about selling yourself is that you are already an expert on you. Once you're aware of this, you can then begin seeking out how to build meaningful business relationships that can lead to those million-dollar sales conversations.

Successful Sales Start with Conversations That Lead to Relationships

When I was younger, I had a number of sales jobs. I went door-to-door selling, and I realized something very important. Making a sale all started with creating a conversation that would engage my prospect in a meaningful way. Sometimes these conversations led to meaningful relationships, and other times they didn't. When one human being makes an honest attempt to engage with another for purposes that transcend selling, the relationship will have a stronger bond.

Ultimately, the more opportunities you create for conversations, the more chances you have to build meaningful relationships. Creating meaningful relationships is one of the essential keys to developing a million-dollar sales conversation. Each successful sales opportunity starts with a conversation—learn about your prospects and what *matters* to them.

Everyone has different needs and wants. Learning each prospect's specific motivations is the only way to provide true value. Your value is not determined by you and then pitched to your prospect. Your conversations with a prospect should be give and take, with both of you staying engaged in and benefiting from the discussion. If your prospects don't think there is value in what you're saying or doing, they aren't going to buy what you're selling. Similarly, if you don't believe in the value of what you're saying or doing, how can you expect someone else to believe you, let alone buy from you?

I always think about what I can do for my prospects. I work to provide them with value first so they can see that what I do is more about them than myself. I show them that I care more about what they need rather than what I want or need. This may be easier said than done. So how do you do it? Maintain your focus when talking to prospects. Make sure you stay motivated. The best way to do this is to put yourself in your prospect's shoes. Concentrate on how you come across in conversations, and be aware of your word choices. Your conversations should focus on figuring out a prospect's needs and wants, not on overcoming his or her objections. Make sure you're asking questions that matter, and that show you're on the same page as your prospect. Test him or her for reactions, and paraphrase what he or she has said to you and repeat it back to the person to show you truly do understand his or her concerns. This is what it takes to be in a million-dollar conversation.

In the book *Networlding: Building Relationships and Opportunities for Success*, Melissa Giovagnoli Wilson and Jocelyn Carter-Miller focus on the value of being a giver first when you begin a new relationship. The idea is that all of us have our own "networld," which includes the people from all areas of your life with whom you are connected through intents, values, interests, and goals. From here it involves creating *exchanges* in the form of conversations where you offer support to others who, in turn, work with you, buy from you and refer you to others because they trust that you will have the same vibrant conversations.

"The essence of Networlding is its appeal to our inherent connectedness to each other and passion for our causes," Giovagnoli and Carter-Miller write. "The connectedness and passion create fertile ground for developing new opportunities that lead to success and rewards of deep, personal fulfillment."

Be a Giver First

Think for a moment how you react when someone you don't know approaches you. Your immediate reaction is probably something along the lines of, "Oh, great, what does he/she want from me?" We are all taught at a very young age to never talk to strangers. Instinctively, our first reaction is to protect ourselves when we see someone we don't know coming over to talk to us. Our guard is up. We build an internal wall of protection.

How do you become a giver when you don't know someone or you have never talked to him or her? One great way to break through is to offer the person a true compliment. The compliment has to be genuine and has to come across from the heart. Getting a compliment from someone makes you feel good and interested in interacting. Every day we are doing things for other people and reacting to everything that is happening to us. When you compliment people, it causes them to pause and think about something positive. It is a great way to break the ice. Compliments can be about anything—clothes, kids, houses, pictures and so forth. You get the point. You need to find something to break the ice. Your goal is to make a connection with them quickly to get past their automatic defensive systems.

We have all been at a store when the first salesperson who sees us trots over and asks, "How can I help you?" Consider how different your reaction would be if that same person started out offering you a compliment. Would you be more open to a conversation? Once you have established some rapport, you then have an opportunity to start asking questions that relate to your prospect's needs. Here's an example. The other day I was walking through a large retail store when a salesperson approached me. To my surprise, he chose to ask me something different than the usual "How can I help you?" He asked if he could point me in the right direction. I paused for a moment and said, "Yes, I'm looking for the kid's section." Instead of pointing me to the kid's section, he walked me there and asked me if I had kids. I immediately started talking about my three kids. Of course, that put me in a great mood; I was talking about my favorite people in the world.

In another example, I recently walked into a department store in search of a white dress shirt with a button-down collar. I was standing up in a wedding the following day. I found the last one in my size, but there was no price tag on it. I grabbed the shirt, took it up to the counter, and asked the clerk for a price. The clerk grabbed it, scanned it, and told me it was $49.99. He proceeded to turn around and walk away to help another customer. At this point, I was more than a little annoyed. I left without buying the shirt.

Here's another example. The other day I saw a lady slip and fall on the floor. I immediately put my hand out to help her up. In that instant, she knew that my only motivation was for her safety and well-being. I proceeded to help her pick up her belongings, and then I escorted her to her office. These are the kinds of feelings you need to tap into for your contacts and customers to truly build lasting relationships.

Sure, you might be a little wary of people you just meet who claim they want to help you; however, we all have instincts that guide us when we know something doesn't feel right. Typically, something doesn't feel right when someone's actions are inconsistent with his or her words. As a salesperson, our job is to tap into the emotions that allow people to understand our intentions are genuine. People don't walk into stores or call places of business because they aren't interested in buying something. Successful salespeople always have the mindset of helping first and not trying to sell. It starts with the right kind of conversations with contacts and potential customers. As the conversations develop, so does the relationship.

For example, let's say you work in sales for a technology company. A couple comes in and tells you they're not ready to buy; they're just looking. They are in the process of gathering information and understanding what options are available to them. They share that they are building a new home and want to make sure it will be more of a smart house with the latest technology. This is clearly your opportunity to start talking or, more specifically, asking questions so you can help them better. How did they pick their house? How did they choose their home's location? Were they starting a family? How big is their house? How many rooms does it have? What are their hobbies? What kinds of things do their kids like to do? What type of work do they do? How do they envision the house working? If they could have anything they wanted in the house, what would it be?

You have to determine not only what type of technology they need but also what kind of house they have and how they plan on living in that house. You need to understand who they are: active, outgoing, introverts, or travelers. They are very early in the process, so make sure they know you accept that fact and are only asking them questions as a way to offer some free advice.

This is a perfect chance to build on your conversations with them. In fact, they're going about the process the same way most people would. They start at the early stage. The more time you invest with them and the more you understand who they are, what they want, and how they live, the better you will be able to help them. You may have gone through the same process when you bought your new home and wanted to upgrade it for the latest technology. This is a great opportunity to make a connection and share a story to find some common ground with them. Suddenly, you have something upon which to build a relationship.

Most salespeople view the early stages of the sales process as a very hard time because the customer isn't ready to make a purchase. They don't want to waste their time or spin their wheels if the sale isn't going to happen for three to six months. They pass up these million-dollar opportunities. These are the salespeople that never last because they're looking for quick fixes and instant gratification.

After about two weeks, you should pick up the phone and give that couple a call to see how the new home building is going. Ask them about something you uncovered during your first conversation. You'll be giving yourself another chance to expand the relationship while checking in with them. During the process, you're also reminding them of new technologies in the marketplace and that you're still interested in trying to help them accomplish their goals. Just the fact that you're calling to see how things are going with them is beneficial from a selling standpoint. Providing them with relevant information regarding their potential purchase will add value to the conversation and show you're going out of your way to help them. It will also show you're not just an order taker.

After two more weeks go by, call them again. After that, they'll be back in your store showing you blueprints and talking about how to implement some of the suggestion you made a while ago. This all started from a conversation. In addition, it's a new development, and they recommend you to all the neighbors. Before you know it, you have 10 referrals in the same neighborhood because of the time you took getting to know one couple. Of course, there was never any guarantee they would come back and buy anything from you, but relationships that are nurtured have the *potential* to bloom much more readily and often than those that are not.

You'll Never Stop Selling

Selling starts much earlier than we realize. Ask yourself, for instance, what you did back in your pre-teen or early teen years. Chances are you probably were involved in some sort of selling. Take the example of my teen years. I started my first business in 1983 when I was thirteen years old. I hosted carnivals on the front lawn with my brother, charging neighborhood kids for playing games, riding motorcycles, and throwing darts and water balloons. Since that time, I have never stopped selling, although the things I've sold have changed periodically. Every time I started selling anything, it always started with a conversation and led to something more. The following year, I opened a car-detailing business on the driveway of my parents' house. I did that for two years. Then in 1986, I started a landscaping company with 3 of my friends, and we ended up with more than 50 homes to service. While I did that, I also delivered pizzas. Then when I was in college, I started a promotional company selling T-shirts, glasses, and a number of other items.

Now you might be wondering what all of these different types of businesses have in common with each other. You may have heard that in order to be successful, you must look around to find a need that isn't being met. Every one of these businesses certainly represents that, but it goes even further than that. The more I became involved in different types of businesses, the more I realized that the most valuable customers were those I had a relationship with.

So I began focusing on learning more about the people I was talking to so that I could mold and build million-dollar conversations. The more I knew about my customers, the easier it was to please them. For example, Mr. Wilson, one of the customers from my car-detailing business, had been a customer for a while. I used to walk our dog every day at the same time, and it just so happened that he walked his dog at that time too, so we struck up a conversation. He ended up getting his car detailed every week, but after he had gotten a new job with a forty-five-minute commute, it was hard for him to leave his car with me. Since I knew that he golfed every Wednesday at 4:00 p.m., I offered to pick up his car at the golf course, take it home, detail it, and then return it to him by the time his golf game was finished. If I hadn't spent the time getting to know him, I would have never realized that I could pick up his car at the golf course. Building a relationship led me to a solution that worked for both of us. He was extremely pleased that I was willing to go the extra mile to help him. Three of his golfing buddies asked me if I would do the same thing for them. I used to bring my car-detailing equipment to the golf course and detail the cars for people there. It worked out for all of us.

Since my carnival and car-detailing days, my selling career hasn't stopped. After I graduated from college, I began working for McHugh Bowles Real Estate, managing thousands of apartment units. Then in 1994, I worked as a trader at the options exchange. Two years later, I became an account manager for CDW, a Fortune 270 company. By 2000, I had moved into management and was working with teams in a variety of different business units and verticals, including those involving small businesses, the government, education, nonprofit organizations, and corporations. I managed businesses in several different states, including Texas and Illinois. I trained more than 750 account managers and mentored more than 30 managers. In addition, I have driven more than $1.7 billion in cumulative sales for CDW. I also have started a number of businesses, including a real estate management company and a pet company. Now I'm the director of sales at Presidio Technologies. And, just like the aforementioned sales examples, my jobs came through strong conversations.

Get In at the Beginning of the Sale—Not the End

Through all of these years of selling, the lesson has been the same. Start with a conversation that leads to a relationship. Look for some commonalities (e.g., you both went to the same school, you both have an interest in football, you both like theatre), and go from there. The key is inserting the personal side and the social side of you at the beginning of the buying process, not the end of it. Multiple studies support this fact. We won't go through all of them, but one of the most interesting is a 2012 study conducted by *Harvard Business Review*. It demonstrates how important it is that we don't relegate ourselves to order takers.

In the study, researchers found that most customers' decisions are almost 60 percent finished before they contact a salesperson. In fact, they discovered that by the time most customers contact a salesperson, they have essentially decided that they're going to do business with someone else. At this point, they're just doing some final benchmarking before signing on the dotted line. They also found that average-performing salespeople tended to get in on the back end of deals, while those who were high performing tended to get into deals at the very beginning.

In other words, high-performing salespeople use their social skills to get to know their customers over a long period of time. They build a relationship by gaining the customer's trust and getting in at the beginning of the decision-making process. High-performing salespeople are more than just order takers; they're trusted advisors—customers share valuable intellectual capital with them so the best possible solutions can be found.

Make Yourself the One Salesperson Customers Have Already Chosen

I have seen hundreds of salespeople try to position solutions before understanding anything about their potential customers. They make assumptions and try to move too quickly. This is a huge mistake and usually leads to smaller sales and unhappy customers. Salespeople also make assumptions about whether the prospect is serious or just looking. They don't want to waste time with potential customers who aren't serious. Again, that is another huge mistake. Clearly, every customer is an opportunity, and every salesperson who has an opportunity to interact with a customer should take it seriously.

Each time you have a conversation with a potential customer, you get a chance to know the person better. You also have a chance to set yourself apart and put yourself in a position to truly help him or her. Taking an interest in your customer's goals, objectives, needs, wants, and desires helps you create an environment to build the right solutions.

If you've set the stage for a relationship with potential customers from the very beginning, odds are that you've made them part of the 60 percent—those potential customers who are engaging other salespeople but already planning to buy from you. When people are spending thousands of dollars on technology, they're going to do some due diligence and visit other stores. It's just human nature; however, when you have forged a connection with them—a relationship—they will be back, and they will be sending you referrals and asking you to help their friends and family too.

When I managed apartments for McHugh Bowels Real Estate, I made it my mission to spend time with families so I could really get to know what they needed. It wasn't just about renting apartments. It was about making sure that the right families ended up in the right apartments. That takes time and energy. There's a myriad of problems that can arise if you don't connect the right families with the right apartments. The families could end up breaking their leases early, which isn't good for them or your client. There could also be problems if their lifestyles really conflict with those of the current residents.

Take the Millers, Carol and Dan, for example. When they first came to see Angela, a million-dollar sales conversation artist, they were newlyweds in search of their first apartment together. At the time, they were living in his apartment, but they wanted to find a new place that didn't feel just like his apartment. Initially, they were so concerned with price that they were looking for a one-bedroom place, but after getting to know them a bit, Angela found out that they were really looking forward to starting a family. She didn't dive right into the process immediately. She took a few months to find the right place. This ended up being a very good thing because it didn't take long for Carol Miller to become pregnant—with twins. By working with them over a longer period of time, Angela was able to find them a three-bedroom apartment they could easily afford on their budget.

The lesson? Don't be in a rush to close a deal because circumstances could quickly change during the buying process that would make your client's needs change.

Practice Getting to Know Others

You can't get to know potential customers overnight. This is the sort of thing that comes with time and practice. You may consider starting with the people you already know. Believe it or not, there are probably many things you don't already know about them. In fact, you may discover a common interest upon which you both can build.

You can also try various exercises to hone your skills for getting to know people. One of my colleagues who trains salespeople asks them to pair up with someone they know. This is especially great for companies that want to improve the skills of their sales force.

If you have a group of sales professionals, try this exercise. Have people pair up and ask questions of each other, back and forth, so that they can learn about the things they have in common. When doing the exercise, find out if you both like to read, golf, or travel. Look for that common interest. In all likelihood, the things you share in common will surprise you.

In one case, two partners in a law firm were surprised to discover that they both had been playing the cello since childhood. Even though they had been partners for over 20 years, they never knew about their mutual passion for the instrument. This commonality was the bridge to a new layer of communication for them.

And it may not be limited to just common interests. Perhaps you both have children who are about the same age. Maybe the person you pair up with is facing a challenge that you can help with in some way. If you both like to read, talk about the types of books you both like and what you're reading at the moment. And then there is always sports. People can find amazing things to talk about with each other when they just learn what they have in common. The search for commonalities with others will help you establish relationships you can build on. In the process, you can create not only powerful connections for the present but also *opportunities* upon which you can build for the future. This "opportunity-expansive" outcome has happened again and again as a result of starting with million-dollar conversations.

Warren Buffett and Bill Gates met on July 5, 1991. As it turns out, both were part of each other's networks. Why? Buffett knew Katharine Graham, who at the time was chairman of the *Washington Post*. She talked him into attending a get-together with her friend Meg Greenfield, who was also an editor at the *Post*. Greenfield knew Bill Gates' mother, who convinced him to attend.

At first glance, the two didn't have much in common. A 2008 article in the *Financial Times* that chronicles this meeting indicates that Buffett was less than thrilled about it. He told Alice Schroeder that during the long drive to the Gates' home, he had asked, "What the hell are we going to spend all day doing with these people? How long do we have to stay to be polite?" And Gates apparently had similar feelings. Another article in the *Harvard Business Review* quotes him as asking, "What were he and I supposed to talk about? P/E ratios?"

But Buffett was introduced to Gates and dove right in, not even bothering with small talk. He asked Gates about IBM and whether the company was competing with Microsoft and if it would do well going forward. He asked why computer companies didn't seem to last long, and Gates started to explain why. He then told the "Oracle of Omaha," who earned the nickname for his visionary stock purchases, that he should buy Microsoft and Intel shares.

And right there, the two had found a connection. From there, Gates asked Buffett about the newspaper business, and Buffett admitted that other forms of media were creating too much competition. They ended up talking so much that they practically ignored everyone else who was at the party. At that first meeting, Gates tried to sell Buffett a computer. Mind you, he's not a salesman—at least not in the traditional sense, as Steve Ballmer became known more as the salesman at Microsoft, while Gates was the techie guy. Buffett didn't bite then, but he uses a computer on a regular basis now to do something both he and Gates enjoy—playing bridge.

Years later, Buffett built on his relationship with Gates by getting him interested in playing online bridge. Gates apparently learned how to play the game from his parents, but it wasn't until he met Buffett that he really became passionate about it. Today, they still play together. In 2005, they got together to start a bridge program in public schools, donating $1 million in funds to get that program started. However, that program has ended.

In 2010, the two billionaires went public with their Giving Pledge Campaign. They wanted to encourage the world's wealthiest people to commit the majority of their wealth to charitable causes.

Since the pledge began, more than 100 people and families have pledged to donate most of their wealth.

Sales Is More than Just Closing the Deal

Successful salespeople aren't just focused on closing the deal. They have time and effort invested in the outcome because they have opened up conversations that lead to relationships, forming bonds with their customers. And the term "salesperson" doesn't apply only to people who consider themselves to be in the business of selling. As I have pointed out, everyone has something to sell. It's all about *initiative.*

At the age of thirteen, my friend and I started a landscaping business, and we ended up having over 50 lawns that we would cut during the summer. We also trimmed hedges and bushes, planted flowers, and so forth. We kept that business through high school. We had to manage the books, the profits, the customers, and the workers. This was a great business, and we were bringing in more than $20,000 a summer.

After we had graduated from high school, we sold the business for over $50,000. I went off to college and started another business, this time making T-shirts and glassware. Again, this was an opportunity for me to sell door-to-door in the college dorms. I also decided at this time to sell candy. This turned into a great opportunity to meet all the kids in the school as well as make some money. It eventually led to some great relationships, too.

As I got older, I realized that it wasn't about the money. It was about the challenge, the connection to others, and the desire to help people. I liked the satisfaction I got from providing a service to people and building relationships in the process. I also knew that talking to people and being able to provide a service was a great way to make a living.

Before college, I had a variety of jobs. I also delivered pizza at night and got to meet many people in the neighborhood. This was during the time I ran the landscaping business. Again, I was always meeting people and being active. I also promoted, organized, and hosted parties where we charged people an entrance fee. In addition, I worked waiting tables at the local Olive Garden for a summer, and I worked at Gillette Stadium, home of the New England Patriots, when selling beer there was difficult.

After college, I continued to develop my sales skills. My first job was working as a landlord in Chicago managing buildings, collecting rent, evicting people, and handling the leasing. I also started a vending-machine company because none of the buildings I managed had a way for the residents to get food or drinks after hours without leaving the premises. This was a great business because it kept the kids and parents from having to go out late at night in areas that weren't completely safe. It truly was something they appreciated.

As you can see, I've held sales positions in numerous industries. The process I've developed for bringing myself and others into million-dollar sales conversations transcends industries. In the rest of this book, we'll identify the building blocks necessary for you to create your own million dollar conversations.

Great Questions to Open Up a Conversation

- What brings you to this event?
- Where are you from?
- What do you like doing when you are not working?
- What is going on in your professional life right now that really excites you?
- What is your favorite part of your job?
- What's the most satisfying project you have worked on recently?

CHAPTER 2
The Attitude of a Conversation

	Have you ever had a conversation with someone who had a great attitude?
	How did that conversation go?
	How did you feel about that conversation?
	How engaged were you in that conversation?
	What did you think about that person?
	Did you want to spend more or less time with that person?

So what is the bottom line here? You need to teach yourself to be positive at all times. In other words, it's all about your attitude. As Winston Churchill once said, "Attitude is a little thing that makes a big difference."

But let's explore this idea further to get more clarity. I'll start with a recent experience I had. I was talking with one of my newer account managers who had only been with the company for about two years. He was struggling to hit his performance numbers. He said the following during our conversation: "I never seem to catch a break. I see everyone around me getting large sales opportunities from customers, big deals from our partners, but it's not happening to me. I'm working all of these accounts and customers, I make fifty to seventy-five calls a day, and I feel like I'm just spinning my wheels."

As we continued the discussion, I asked him what he felt his teammates were doing differently. He said, "I really can't tell. All I see is them laughing and smiling a lot more than me when they are talking to their customers."

"Do you think that might be something you could try with your customers?" I said.

"Try what?"

"Smiling and laughing with your customers."

He looked at me and smiled. At that moment, I think the light bulb went off in his head and he realized that he was always so serious with his customers. He was always focused on making sales. His attitude was constantly about business with his customers; therefore, he was not relating to them on any other level then business. He realized his attitude *about* connecting was preventing him from connecting *effectively*.

A Lesson about Attitude

I'm sure you have heard this before—people buy from people they like. People like having conversations, relating to others and building connections. People with whom you do business are just people, like you. Your attitude about your interactions with people is a lot more than just about the current agenda at hand. You will build strong and lasting relationships by having conversations that *engage* other people. You have to develop a positive attitude in your interactions with others because they can feel and see when you are sincere.

How can you make sure you show up effectively? Prepare. Take time each day to prepare your attitude to be *responsive* rather than *reactive*. Whether it's telling yourself in a mirror every morning, "You're great! You're great! You're great!" or listening to motivational podcasts or reading inspirational passages from any number of books, I guarantee you that these practices will make you smile, and they will also change your attitude. It's just like former president Thomas Jefferson said: "Nothing can stop the man with the right mental attitude from achieving his goal; nothing on earth can help the man with the wrong mental attitude."

I used to work with an account manager named Sam. When asked how he was doing, he would always say, "Super fantastic!" Sam had a great attitude, and his customers always wanted to talk with him. They were happy to call and work with him because he was always extremely happy and cheerful. People have no desire to work with people who aren't upbeat—even unhappy people like to work with upbeat people. As a result, building a positive attitude becomes essential to creating million-dollar conversations.

Think about your attitude. How do you come across to others? Don't take a guess. Instead, ask people you know over the next couple of days the following question: "How do I normally come across to you and others?" Be willing to listen to their responses. See if there are any improvements you can make in the way you show up.

Your attitude can make all the difference in the world. Anthony K. Tjan wrote in the *Harvard Business Review* about what he, Richard Harrington, and Tsun-yan Hsieh found in their study about entrepreneurial luck. They discovered that those who are humble, curious, and optimistic tend to go much further than those who are not.

It's important to have enough self-confidence that new contacts will trust you; it's also important to be humble about the things you don't know. Humility humanizes you to the people you meet, and Tjan calls it "the path towards earning respect." He also says that it's the basis for the second important trait, which is intellectual curiosity.

While there is an intellectual component to curiosity, there is a human component that exists inside our relationships. Being curious about your new contacts enables you to get to know them. Be inquisitive about their families, jobs, interests, and anything else that will help you discover a commonality upon which you can build your relationship.

Finally, being an optimist is usually a self-fulfilling prophecy. In his *Harvard Business Review* article, Tjan referred to optimism as "the energy source to allow for positive change." If you believe good things can happen, they are more likely to happen because you aren't placing negative mental roadblocks in your own path. You may be telling yourself that you're just not someone who's naturally optimistic, but believe it or not, optimism is something that can be learned.

In his book, *It Worked for Me*, retired four-star general Colin Powell talks about how important it is to have a positive attitude—whether you're in the trenches or on the sales floor. He said the positive attitude habit was drilled in him at the Infantry School. He graduated thinking, "Things will get better. You will make them get better."

As a salesperson, it's up to you to make things better, for both yourself and your customers. In addition to being positive all the time, another part of that winning attitude means putting others first at all times—something else that was drilled into Powell in military training. A positive attitude and putting others first go hand-in-hand because others will take cues from your attitude, one way or another.

"Lieutenant, you may be starving, but you always eat last," Powell wrote. "You may be freezing or near heat exhaustion, but you must never show that you are cold or hot. You may be terrified, but you must never show fear. You are the leader and the troops will reflect your emotions."

If you're positive, your customers will be positive. If you're putting them first, they will pick up on the fact that you're not just looking out for yourself. On the other hand, if your assumption is that you have to be on the defensive because people are looking to take advantage of you, you are not going to be successful. You can't go in with the attitude that you *need* to protect yourself. If people sense that you're only looking out for yourself, you won't get to the next level. Instead of looking out for yourself, you should be looking out for your customers in the same way a lieutenant looks after his troops.

Partner-Building Attitude

When you're looking out for the needs of your customers, it's important to realize that they are *people* first, even when they represent a large company. The best relationship you can have with them is that of a partner. But how do you get to that level? Take a look at the framework below and think about how you can adjust your attitude to build a supportive and mutually beneficial relationship with your customers.

Be the following:

- Responsive instead of reactive
- Curious instead of assumptive
- Collaborative instead of self-focused
- Helpful instead of compliant
- Appreciative instead of expecting
- Happy instead of annoyed

When a prospect asks you to do something, he or she is testing you. The way you respond to his or her request will help determine your ability to cultivate a positive or negative relationship.

Whenever it is possible, you should say something like, "It would be my pleasure to do that."

Customers often put their defenses down when you agree to their requests because they feel a personal connection—one of friendship. You should always aim for that kind of connection, even if you think you're not going to get a sale out of it.

Again, this goes back to your attitude about helping. You need to have a clear attitude that your objective is to help your customers/contacts, and you need to be happy about them giving you an opportunity. Clearly, there's a reason a contact is asking you for help. Even if you believe he or she is testing you, you need to pass this test. You only have one opportunity to make a good first impression, and this will set you apart from 95 percent of the people. Therefore, your goal should be to build a relationship by giving 100 percent, regardless of whether you think you'll be getting a sale.

Mary Kay Ash, founder of Mary Kay Cosmetics, provided the following advice to her salespeople: "Pretend that every single person you meet has a sign around his or her neck that says, 'Make me feel important.' Not only will you succeed in sales, you will succeed in life." This is a surefire way to build relationships with contacts and customers. Next, move your relationships with contacts into the personal zone. Creating personal relationships with contacts will take you from being a salesperson, supplier, or vendor into the inner circle of partnerships where million-dollar conversations happen.

When to Say No

You may be thinking, "There have to be times when I need to say no to customers. I have to manage my day and prioritize. If I'm always doing things for every customer, I will never get anything done." You're right about that, but you must choose carefully when deciding which customers to say no to and why.

Perhaps the biggest reason to say no is because a customer is taking advantage of you. Give 100 percent and expect nothing in return; however, if you consistently get nothing in return, it may be time for a change. Look for opportunities for *exchange* or appreciation from your customer.

You might also consider saying no if a customer is resisting your help. Sometimes people ask for your help, but they continually refuse to take your advice. In this situation, you are much better spending your time with someone who will appreciate and benefit from your time and knowledge.

Whatever the reason you have for saying no to a customer, be careful about the way you do it. Tap into your emotional connection with your customer and utilize it when talking. Don't make up phony excuses, because the customer will sense what you're doing. Have an honest conversation. Be genuine and sincere. Have the message come from your heart, and look for ways to make it up to him or her the next time.

If you believe a customer has an issue with you, and you're not sure what it is, ask the person about it directly. Perhaps it was something you did, something you said, or something you didn't do. After you get the answer, offer a sincere apology that comes from your heart. You have to truly mean it. Your goal is to bring the person back into the zone where you have a chance to rebuild the relationship. Then move forward and look for the next positive step you can take together.

While it can be tempting to fire a customer, in my experience, it's not a good idea. There is always something you can do to turn a bad relationship into a positive relationship. Do not give up. You never know whom the person may know, where he or she may end up, or when another opportunity may present itself. Take time to reflect. Then re-engage the customer when you have a better mind-set.

Expectations

Mother Teresa said many wonderful and inspiring things while she was alive, but this statement from her captures the essence of what you should strive for in every relationship: "Let no one ever come to you without leaving better and happier." The key to making customers feel better and happier is to cultivate friendships with them so your extensive business knowledge can benefit them on a regular basis. Here are the steps to building solid, long-lasting business relationships from the start:

1. **Create a relationship.** Do this by starting with great conversations.
2. **Personalize the relationship**. Connect by looking for personal things that matter to the person with whom you are connecting.

3. **Cultivate the relationship.** Do little things for your contacts that you know they will like. Spend time with them in a nonbusiness environment.
4. **Sustain the relationship.** Take time at least once a month to touch base with them. Consider sending your connections articles of interest, or just check in to see how they are doing. Also, remember to wish them happy birthday and to congratulate them when it is appropriate.
5. **Expand the relationship.** Stay connected as if they are your friend. Call with no other agenda but to see how they are doing. Invite them to a sporting event or concert.

Your Landscape of Relationships

Not all relationships are the same, and the specific actions you take to build them will vary. For example, the type of birthday card you would send to a friend who likes to joke around with you would be different than the one you would send to a customer who tends to have a more serious disposition. This is why it's important to focus on what type of relationship you're building with each customer. Here is an overview of the types of relationships you can create:

Acquaintances. These are people you might know but with whom you don't cultivate relationships.

Contacts. These are people you talk to occasionally and interact with around specific items or topics where they have expertise. You know them on a business level, or they serve a purpose in your world.

Personal Relationships. These are people you consider friends and interact with regularly. You can count on them to help you, and you would help them. They may or may not turn into customers.

Prospects. If you refer to the connections you make as "prospects," you are in salesperson mode.

Partnerships. These are the best professional relationships. They are also true professional friendships—the best of both worlds, personal and business. You could call these "personalized business relationships."

All Relationships Are Unique—Personalize Them

Personalized business relationships move customers away from being defensive and toward the Million-Dollar Conversation Zone. So, how can you recognize a customer who is being defensive? He or she may use words or phrases that don't provide any substantive responses to your questions. They may even look down when speaking with them and avoid eye contact. They may also not respond to your voicemails or emails. You may initially think that this is just the particular customer you are dealing with, but in reality, it has everything to do with you, your attitude, and the type of energy you're giving off. If you hear this type of phrasing from a new contact, it means the person can recognize your intent—what it is you want from him or her.

Each relationship is going to be different, so don't expect the same results across all of your relationships. It can be tempting to treat every customer the same. Aim for a *personalized business relationship.* This will give you plenty of chances to show that you know your customer extremely well, and you'll be able to tailor your relationship to the wants and needs of each person.

Everyone has different needs and wants; thus, everyone moves at different speeds through the steps of building a relationship with you. You might run through all five relationship-building steps in a matter of weeks or months with one customer, but then you might spend a year or more running through the steps with another customer. Each one of the steps will look different too. Sustaining a relationship with one person may mean having lunch on a regular basis with him or her, while with another, it may mean playing tennis together periodically. With truly personalized relationships, the relationship-building steps I gave you should not look the same every time.

Great salespeople recognize that every interaction is an opportunity to start a conversation that builds, over time, into a solid, personalized relationship. This takes effort, energy, and initiative. Don't wait for the other person to contact you. Create your own opportunities for interactions by reaching out to him or her. For example, check to see how he or she is doing, or call to say that you've found another way to help him or her. If the customer is online, sending them news articles or the occasional news story that is relevant to their interest is a way to stay in touch without being pushy. Many companies do this with newsletters, but make your contact personal. Taking the time to print off or clip a news story and mail it along with a short, handwritten note does wonders for showing you're serious about being helpful.

Contact your customers on a regular basis, especially every two to four weeks after your last contact with them. Thank them for their time, purchase, or whatever it was and remind them that you're still around to help.

If you have a lot of customers, you may be wondering how you're supposed to keep track of all these interactions. Use your phone or computer to keep track of the date of your last contact with each customer. If you're not particularly tech-savvy, use index cards and store them alphabetically by customer name in what is called a "tickle file." Put together your own tickle file by creating a folder for each month of the year, and 31 folders for each day of the month (43 folders total). You'll move those 31 daily folders to the next month as they're emptied. There are also inexpensive tickle file systems you can simply purchase to make it easier to set up. The idea is quite simple: anything you need to be reminded of on some future date goes into your tickler file. Every morning, you pull that day's folder. You then add whatever you placed in the folder days, weeks, or months earlier on your to-do list or in your inbox. That way every day you know exactly who to contact and why, even if it's been months since you first placed the information in your file.

If you want to know more about how tickle files work see David Allen's book, "*Getting Things Done.*"

Include some notes with that date/file so you can remember what you did and talked about. Then schedule yourself a date and time to contact the customer again.

You can also put reminders to contact each customer in the calendar that's on your smartphone so that they will pop up when it's time for you to contact them again. Then refer back to your notes before you make the contact. Store your notes in an easy-to-sort format so that you can easily locate customers by name. There are numerous software programs you can use, so just figure out what works for you, whether it's a database or a Word document, you can search by name.

Remember the five Ps of success: proper planning prevents poor performance. In other words, plan ahead by putting yourself in the mind-set that you are looking to build personalized, long-term relationships so that when you start conversations with contacts, you open up possibilities.

When a customer says, "Please review this proposal your competitor did for me and I'll give you an opportunity to prove your intentions," you have to capitalize on the fact that the customer contacted you. This is your opportunity to show him or her that you're willing to help, even if your efforts might not result in a sale for you. Many times this is a test to see how open and willing to help you truly are.

Contacts will become defensive if they think you're in it for yourself. When a contact becomes defensive, it becomes much more difficult to get him or her to open up. Your goal should be to avoid this uphill battle and not make the customer defensive.

Always Be Authentic

If you're being authentic, the customer won't be defensive. So how do you demonstrate authenticity? Authenticity has to do with being honest, open, and straightforward with people. Your actions need to be consistent with your words.

I have seen salespeople make this error many times. They say one thing and do another. They don't follow up when they say they are going to. They may not call back when they promised. They may even ignore customer calls when they don't have the answers. They never take responsibility for their actions and always point the finger at someone else. Human beings can tell when you aren't being authentic.

One time we were involved with a particular deal, and the customer had already done a lot of work with our competitor. We knew from experience that we were late to the game and would probably lose the sale. A salesperson for our company said, "I don't want to waste my time chasing a deal I know we're going to lose. I really don't think we have a chance."

Because of that mind-set, the sales rep said no to the customer. I said to him later, "Are you thinking about the long-term relationship with the customer, or just this one opportunity?" I went on to ask him, "What do you think the customer wants us to do?"

"I think they want us to confirm they are getting the right solution," the salesperson said.

"What do you think that would do for our long-term relationship with the customer?" I said.

The salesperson looked at me and said, "Don't you think it's obvious? It would help it."

Clearly, the rep had figured out that we needed to take the time to look over the competitor's work and offer our recommendations. We didn't charge the customer to review the work, and we actually found several items in which the competitor had made mistakes. The customer confirmed our recommendations with the manufacturer and was extremely grateful for our assistance. We had proven to the customer that he could trust us because we genuinely wanted to help. Today, this customer is one of our largest accounts in the area.

The sales business is not about selling; it's about working with people and helping them. Sales are a by product of helping people solve their problems. When you start thinking about helping people and forget about selling, you are on your way to the next level.

I'm always baffled when salespeople say to me, "A customer just called for a quote, and I know they already have a price from our competitor. I don't want to give them a price because I know they are just price shopping. Why would I want to do that?"

Why wouldn't they want to do that? The customer is giving them a chance to build a relationship, open a conversation, and *expand* the opportunity by proving they want to be helpful. At times, salespeople are very shortsighted.

A 2007 study conducted for a well-known hotel chain by Dr. Frank Mulhern of Northwestern University demonstrates how a helping attitude usually leads customers to spend more money with the person who helped them. The study linked customer spending habits with the attitudes of hotel employees. Researchers found that the most important thing customers wanted was for the hotel workers to help them. A research paper on the study states the salesperson's attitude shouldn't be that "I am here to sell you this widget." Instead, it should be that "I am here to listen and to see if/how I can be of assistance."

Develop Your Brand

What else can we learn from that research study? It's important to make helping a part of your brand. There have been many articles and books written about how you are a brand. Part of your brand is about how you come across in the very first meeting with the potential customer. Are you helpful and friendly? Are you sloppily dressed? Do you have coffee on your tie?

To test your brand, have a mock meeting with some people you know well and get feedback as to how they perceive you in a business setting. What they say will undoubtedly be revealing. We often pick up bad habits without even realizing that we have done so. We may be thinking one way, but expressing ourselves in the complete opposite direction. This is why it is so important to get feedback from others about how you come across in a meeting.

The strength of your brand and how you come across will enable you to turn a prospect into a long-term relationship and, eventually, into a partner. Once again, you have to have an attitude that you are going to be successful. This is key to achieving that success. This means looking beyond what's in front of you currently to see what's possible in the long-term.

Questions

1. Have you ever dealt with someone who was not prepared?
2. Have you ever dealt with someone with a bad attitude?
3. If the answer to either of those questions is yes, how did it make you feel?
4. What level of confidence do you have in someone who has a positive persona?
5. If you could choose anyone, what type of person would you want to work with on a regular basis?

Putting This Step into Action

1. **Prepare your attitude daily.** Listen to TED talks, read inspirational quotes, or do whatever you need to do. Be responsive rather than reactive. Be curious rather than assumptive. Be collaborative rather than self-focused. Be helpful rather than compliant. Be appreciative rather than expectant. Be happy rather than annoyed.
2. **Make others feel important**. Offer to help people whenever they ask—and even when they don't—with anything they need. Go the extra mile to show that you care enough about them to help even when you may not benefit.
3. **Learn when to say no.** Prioritize your many responsibilities with numerous customers. Push back if you feel a customer is taking advantage of you. Always apologize sincerely, and don't make up fake excuses when you do need to say no, especially in situations when you have a great relationship with a customer but you're simply overbooked.

4. **Aim for personalized business relationships.** Take total responsibility for your relationships by giving without expecting anything in return. Always thank customers for their time, and check in with them often. Cultivate the relationship with simple gestures like sending them a birthday card.

5. **Focus on your brand.** Consider the way you dress and be consistent so that others see what you're all about. Think about your customer's brand as well so that you can demonstrate to them that your brand fits in with their culture.

CHAPTER 3

Seeing the Horizon of Possibility (Opportunity) – Now – Build Your Platform by Setting Goals

	Have you ever set any goals for your life?
	If so, how successful were you at meeting them?
	If you were successful, why do you think that was?
	If you didn't meet your goals, why do you think you didn't?
	What are two goals you would like to set right now?

Goal setting is the key to success in life, not just selling. When I managed our inside sales organization, we always used goal setting as a technique to drive better results. We always provided our new sales reps daily activity goals. We knew that setting daily goals would lead to hitting weekly goals, then monthly goals, and yearly goals. We always set the expectation and provided the data to support the results.

Let me give you an example of how we set goals with the new reps. We would show them their yearly quota and work backward, breaking it down to a daily numbers. Each new sales rep coming into the organization was expected to produce $2.4 million in revenue and $240,000 in gross profits. This was a yearly number that looked rather large and could be quite intimidating to a new salesperson. However when we broke this down to a monthly number, then a daily number, it became an achievable, manageable goal. We also broke down the daily activity needed to hit those weekly and monthly goals. We determined the number of calls, quotes, close ratio, and the average order size. We used historic data to demonstrate that an average rep made 100 calls a day, did 20 quotes a day, and closed 20% of their quotes. The average order size was $2,500. If the rep stuck with the daily goals they would close 4 orders a day and average $10,000 a day in sales. That would translate into $50,000 a week, or $200,00 a month in sales with an average margin of 10%, that would equal $20,000 a month in profit. Now during these conversations with the reps, we knew that no new rep came into the organization to be average. So if an average rep was doing the above, we asked them what did they think they could do above and beyond that. We established the baseline and let the individual account managers set their goals based off that baseline. Every single one of the new reps always set goals above the baseline. They never wanted to be average. Each year the results would exceed the prior year, and the averages would continue to rise. That meant that each year our conversations about averages would increase with each new rep. Here is a great example of how goal setting works to drive activity and results.

Many salespeople come to me and ask for tips about how they can boost their sales performances. I simply tell them that they have to set some short-term goals. Setting goals makes the job more exciting and fun. It brings out the competitiveness in a salesperson as they work hard to try to soar beyond what they ever thought they could do.

Let me give you an example. It was November. The weather had just changed for the worst and the temperature had dropped by 20 degrees. The gusty, downtown Chicago winds made our eyes water as the group I was walking with struggled through the bitterly cold air. We were definitely experience *The Windy City* of Chicago! We also happened to be in our 4th quarter at CDW and trying to finish the year up strong. Typically, the fourth quarter was our busiest time of the year. That quarter's results would either ensure that we hit our goals for the year or that we missed our annual objective. The prior 10 months were a bit like a roller coaster, some months significantly above goal while others were significantly below. We had 45 days to make up 3% percent or an additional 6-million dollars in revenue.

In addition, we had to do $30 million in sales in those 2 months to hit goal. I had to get the team rallied around this objective and provide them some additional motivation to go the extra mile in the last 45 days of the year. One of things that I did was find a manager with whom I could place a bet to get the two teams competing against each other.

We brought both teams into a room and asked them how they felt about putting a wager in place until the end of year. Of course, the teams all rallied around a little friendly competition. To make it even more interesting, we had a little wager. The bet would be on the performance of the team in the last 45 days and would be measured by which team produced the highest goal attainment. One thing about salespeople is that they are very competitive by nature.

We put our sales goals on the board and said, "Whoever finishes the highest percentage over goal for the month, the other team had to clean all the snow off the other teams cars and warm them up. Having just walked through the bitter wind and cold to the office, each team knew exactly what they were agreeing to. This was a serious bet. The competition was for the entire first week in January." This was the perfect way to motivate and spark our teams in Chicago.

The energy in the room erupted with excitement. The trash talking started immediately and went on for the entire 45 days. The teams would check the numbers every day, tracking their performance, checking on each other, and making sure that everyone was doing their part. They were all holding each other accountable for their performance. They were totally invested in this competition and were working together to achieve their goals. No one on either team wanted to lose, they all wanted their cars cleaned and warmed up. Not only would they win a clean, warm car, they'd get bragging rights for the entire quarter, even the year. As a result, we achieved our two highest monthly goals, adding another six million on top of our original goal! The team was being very creative around driving the year-end numbers.

See what can happen when you set goals? Goal setting is the key to success in life, not just selling. But the big problem for many people is that they set goals they either can't or never intend to meet. For example, did you know that 25 percent of those who set New Year's resolutions abandon them just a week after they set those goals? In fact, 60 percent of them dump their resolutions entirely within 6 months. Also, the average person makes the same New Year's resolution 10 different times without finding success. So what do these statistics tell us about setting goals? They tell us that not only is it very difficult to meet our goals, but few people achieve them even when they do set them. Those who do achieve their goals may be in the minority, but it's possible.

What Does it Take to Successfully Set Goals?

Tony Robbins said, "Setting goals is the first step in turning the invisible into the visible." So how can we really turn what's invisible into real visible results in our own lives? First, I've found that you have to want to be more successful than you want to breathe. That's right. You've got to want success so badly that you cannot only taste it, but that you need it in order to survive. If you've felt this kind of passion in the past, then you know what I'm talking about, but if you haven't, then you may not be setting the right goals. Any goal you set should be something you deeply care about. It's a passion that transcends words.

Second, realize that you can always make excuses and that it's far too easy to do so. Maybe you're taking a break on your diet or whatever it is because you want to go out with friends or you don't want to take the time and put in the extra effort to get to know the contacts you're meeting with. Perhaps you think you deserve a break. You may think others aren't being fair to you and that you need a break to get ahead. You may even be making excuses right now as you're reading this. But as George Washington Carver once said, "99 percent of the failures come from people who have the habit of making excuses." Are you in that 99 percent? Stop for a minute right now and think about why you haven't met the goals you've set for yourself recently. If you think for a moment, you'll probably see an excuse written into every single one of them.

Third, successful goal setters *write their goals down*. It's not enough to *set* goals. You've got to see them in black and white in front of your eyes. If you don't take the time to write them down, then it becomes too easy to forget about them, ignore them, or just plain abandon them entirely.

5 Reasons You Should Set Goals—and <u>Write Them Down!</u>

Let's start by talking about why it's important to write your goals down. Imagine for a moment that you're setting out on a trip. You decide not to set a destination because you think it's more adventurous to see where you end up. As a result, you end up driving in circles after you leave the house, wandering around, but not really ending up anywhere. Finally, you decide that you'd like to head to Florida, so you get on the highway. However, you get off the highway just an hour into your trip because you got distracted by the billboard advertising the world's biggest ball of string and you just had to see it.

When you finally approach the halfway mark of your trip, you realize that you didn't pack the right clothing for your trip. In fact, because you failed to plan ahead, you didn't bring anything at all! So you consider turning back, but decide to keep on going. When you reach the Florida state border, you're unsure which road to take to find a place to stay. The problems you encounter are endless, simply because you didn't set any goals about your trip before you left.

Metaphorically speaking, does any of this sound familiar? Most people who try and fail to meet their goals deal with at least one, if not all of these issues. To circumvent failure and all of these struggles it helps to know why you're setting your goals.

1. **Setting goals forces you to clarify what you want.** Without knowing your destination, you can't make progress toward getting what you want. You can't go grocery shopping for what you need to prepare a meal if you don't know what you're cooking. You won't be able to choose the right roads to take because you don't know where you're going. You can't make plans to ensure that you have what you need when you finally arrive if you don't know where you're going. And then there's the issue of knowing when you have arrived. If you never set goals, how do you know that you've finally been successful? You can't. Not unless you write down your goals. Written goals force you to think things through. Goals help us define and decide which choices to make when faced with multiple opportunities.

2. **Setting goals motivates you to take action.** Writing your goals down is only the beginning. Writing your goals down does require you to articulate your intention, however, articulating it isn't enough. This is where I disagree with Rhonda Byrne, author of _The Secret_. Her premise is that if you want good things to happen to you, then you must think good thoughts. I believe thinking will only get you so far. You must execute and act on your goals if you want to actually achieve anything. I have found that writing down my goals and reviewing them regularly provokes me to take the next most important action to move toward achieving my goal. It lists each step I need

to take to reach the next milestone. Reading the goals you have written down not only reminds you of where you want to go, it consistently whets your appetite for success. Being motivated to reach your goals spurs you on toward the thing you want most—that representation of your million-dollar conversation. If you don't feel motivated to take action, then you'll just end up driving in circles without really going anywhere.

3. **Setting goals also provides a filter for other opportunities.** I've found that the more successful I have become, the more I've been inundated with opportunities. While endless opportunities seem like and can be a great thing, a lot of them can quickly become distractions that pull you off course. It's like the world's biggest ball of string. If you're on a road trip to Florida, that's probably just one of countless sites you may have the opportunity to see, but can or should you stop at every single one? Of course not. If you do, you'll never to make it to Florida, or if you do finally make it there, it will be well after the timeline that you originally planned to follow. Unless your goal is to see every roadside attraction between where you are and Florida, the only antidote I know to avoid distractions is to have a list of goals written down. When you clearly see your goal in front of you it's easy to steer clear of opportunities which are actually distractions rather than stepping stones. By maintaining a list of written goals by which to evaluate new opportunities you can quickly determine whether to stop or pass it by. If the opportunity doesn't serve a purpose in moving you closer to your goal, then pass on it and look for the next one. Unexpected opportunities can speed up your progress, but most will just slow it down by distracting you.

4. **Setting goals helps you overcome resistance.** Every meaningful intention, dream, or goal encounters resistance. From the moment you set a goal, you will begin to feel the resistance. You're not alone. We all have habits that can keep us from meeting our goals. These can range from fear to procrastination, self-doubt, and numerous other "Resistance Points," as Steven Pressfield calls them in his book, _Do the Work_. But if you focus on the resistance, it will only get stronger. "The enemy is our chattering brain, which, if we give it so much as a nanosecond, will start producing excuses, alibis, transparent self-justifications, and a million reasons why we can't/shouldn't/won't do what we know we need to do," Pressfield wrote. The way to overcome it is to focus on the goal—the thing you want. You'll need to get out of your brain to move past the Resistance Point and move into action.

5. **Setting goals enables you to see—and celebrate—your progress**. Life is hard. It is particularly difficult when you aren't seeing much, if any, progress. You may feel like you are working yourself to death, but getting nowhere. Written goals are like mile-markers on a highway. They enable you to see how far you have come and how far you need to go, no matter how you feel about your progress. They are your reality check. They also provide an opportunity for celebration when you attain them. You should have benchmarks along the way to meeting your goal so that you can see how much progress you have made and reward yourself each time you reach a milestone. This isn't indulgence; it's often the only motivation we have. I've found that all we often need to keep going is to stop, take stock of where we are and how far we have come,

and then look forward to see how much further we have to go. There is strength and hope in seeing how much the distance from our beginning to our goal has been reduced!

Figure Out Your Goals

By this point, you're probably excited about what your future holds, but how do you know what your goals should be? They should be based on your million-dollar conversation. Do you know what your million-dollar conversation looks like? As I've said before, it looks like different things to different people. Your million-dollar conversation is the one that opens up the door to the thing you are most passionate about—whatever that passion is. You may even be aiming for more than one million-dollar conversation. Let me tell you about someone I worked with named Tom. In Tom's mind, there was no question about what he wanted.

Tom came from Sears where he was working as a floor manager and making about $30,000 a year. During our interview, he told me drove over 90 minutes a day each way to and from work. He estimated he was working more than 70 hours a week. Tom told me that one of his biggest goals in life was to get married, start a family, and buy a house. He said that he wanted to make enough money to provide for his family and spend time with them, but he wasn't sure how that was possible given his current schedule.

As we started working together and developing our strategy on how to be a successful sales person, I asked him where he thought he needed the most help. He mentioned three areas: developing his product knowledge, improving his sales skills, and building his business acumen. I said to him, "What's your time frame on buying a house, getting married, and starting a family?" I said, "do you have a girlfriend now? Are you engaged? Where are you living now?" He laughed and said, "yes, I have a girlfriend, we aren't engaged, and we live with my parents. I plan on getting engaged as soon as I can; I don't want to let her get away."

I said, "How much do you want to make before you can get engaged and buy a house?" He said, "my goal is $75,000."

Now, in Tom's story there are several goals that were set, discussed, and agreed upon. Tom determined all the goals. Each goal had to do with asking the questions and having a conversation about what was important to him. On a personal level it was clear, he wanted to get married, start a family, and buy a house. On a financial level, he wanted to make $75,000.

The reason it was important that Tom come up with all of his goals on his own is because that created his buy-in and his commitment to each goal. Telling people what their goals should be is very difficult to do. Setting sales quotas is one thing, but that's not going to create you buy-in. That is going to create compliance only. If you've ever been told that your goal was something that you didn't really want to do, then you know how easy it is to lose interest in pursuing it. The only way you will stay motivated and engaged is if you set your own personal goals based on what you really want, just as Tom did.

But what if you're not sure what your goals should be? It's possible you've been aiming for the wrong things for much of your life, chasing someone else's goals for you. Maybe it's your parent's dreams, or your spouse's, or your social circle. Determining whether you've been chasing the wrong goals is pretty easy to do. Inspirational speaker Tony Robbins said those who are going after the wrong goals have "impotent goals, that is, goals that do not inspire them."

One of the most amazing stories I've heard about knowing what you want is the story of Phil Robertson, the patriarch for the reality show "Duck Dynasty." What many people, including viewers, don't know about Phil is that he was a college football star who played ball with NFL great, Terry Bradshaw. It was the late 1960s in Ruston, Louisiana at a school called "Louisiana Tech." There were two standout quarterbacks on that team, Terry Bradshaw, who went on to attain the top pick in the 1970 NFL Draft, a lengthy career with the Pittsburgh Steelers, four Super Bowl victories, a spot in the Hall of Fame, and a second career in front of the camera, and Phil Robertson. Robertson was ahead of Bradshaw on Louisiana Tech's depth chart. He was the starting quarterback, Bradshaw was second-string.

Had Robertson continued to play football we might never have heard the name "Terry Bradshaw." But Robertson knew what he wanted and he wasn't' about to be distracted by football fame and fortune. Robertson gave up football with one year of eligibility remaining because football and any future he might have had in the game, interfered with his heart's dearest passion, duck-hunting. Many of us might say he was crazy, giving up the opportunity to make millions right out of college so he could go duck hunting. What impresses me most about this story is that Robertson knew what he wanted and he pursued it no matter what others thought or said. He was willing to take the harder road to do what he truly wanted to do. Now, he's not only a multi-millionaire several times over, he's still doing what he loves—duck hunting—and he's making a living at it with his television show, "Duck Dynasty."

What inspires you doesn't have to be something as grand as CEO of a billion-dollar company, becoming a star quarterback, or a famous rock star. It can be something as simple as duck hunting, or taking beautiful photos, or helping disadvantaged youth, getting married, or raising a family. Figure out what inspires you. Start by thinking about what you spend most of your time doing, or want to spend more time doing. Time is your most valuable commodity, so where you spend it will probably give you an idea about where you should be. If this isn't the case, then consider what you spend most of your time thinking about. Sometimes we work so much just to pay the bills that we lose sight of what we really want—except it never really leaves our thoughts, not if we really want it. What do you daydream about? What gets your attention when people are talking about their own lives?

As you think about what inspires you, it's helpful to break it down into the two important areas of goal-setting: the personal piece (getting to know someone) and the financial piece (the business side). If you're not sure about both of these areas, that's OK. Just pick the one you're sure about and start working on it.

If you are one of the lucky ones like Tom or Phil Robertson who already knows everything you want and are pursuing it, that's great. Then it's time to move on to the next step. If you're not sure what you want, then you've got some soul searching to do. Believe me, it's worth the time to figure out what you want. Great things wait for those who do! But in the midst of your soul searching, when you do figure out at least one goal, don't neglect it just because it's only one part of the puzzle. That's nothing but an excuse. Start working on that one piece and you just may figure out the rest of the pieces along the way.

Make Addressing Your Goals a Daily Habit

After you've figured out where your passions really lie, then it's time to create and write down the goals you have for them. Writing them down will make it easier for you to address them daily. Your goals should be very specific and measurable. Often the acronym SMART is used: specific, measurable, achievable, relevant, and time-bound.

Many authors have described the SMART acronym through the years, and you may have heard slight variations in what each of those letters stands for. Peter Drucker may be the most well-known author to have referenced SMART goals in his management by objectives idea. However, the acronym can originally be traced back to an article by George T. Doran in the November 1981 issue of *Management Review.*

In that article, the 'A' stood for "assignable," and the 'R' stood for "realistic." Realistic and achievable are both very similar terms, so this idea was in the original acronym, just under a different term. The term assignable deals with management, so if you're a manager creating goals for your team, that acronym might be helpful for you. For the purposes of this book though, we'll focus on individuals and use this acronym: specific, measurable, achievable, relevant, and time-bound. Another author to use this form of the acronym is Paul J. Meyer in his book, *Attitude is Everything.*

The reason for these guidelines is simple. Goals that are too vague are difficult to keep, and they certainly aren't measurable. How do you know when you've made progress toward your goal if you can't measure it? Unmeasurable goals can be a source of frustration because you can't see how far you have come. You don't really know if you're moving toward your goal, or spinning your wheels and staying in place. If you set the bar too high, it's easy to get frustrated as well. Having a timeline in which you want to achieve your goals is helpful because it's part of the measurement process.

In addition to the SMART acronym, it's also a good idea to set short-term milestones on the way to your long-term goals. Break down those longer goals into smaller steps or milestones, and set a time frame in which you want to achieve each milestone. Then, get moving!

Post your goals in a place where you see them every day. Share them with someone who will hold you accountable for meeting those goals. Providing a weekly progress report will give you even more motivation for meeting your goals. If this all sounds like a lot of work, then maybe you should rethink your goals to see if they really reflect what you are truly passionate about.

If you're positive that the goals you've set really reflect what you want, then stop telling yourself that writing them down won't make a difference in whether you meet them or not. It's scientific fact that setting goals and writing them down really does make a difference in whether or not you will meet your goals There is conclusive evidence which shows that the more of these steps you take, the more likely you are to be able to achieve the goals you have set.

Dr. Gail Matthews, a psychology professor at Dominican University in California, did a study on goal-setting with 267 participants between the ages of 23 and 72. She gathered subjects from a variety of businesses, networking groups, and organizations in the U.S. and overseas. She found that people are 42 percent more likely to achieve their goals just by writing them down.

To come up with these results, she grouped people into five groups. She asked Group One to just think about the goals they wanted to accomplish within the next four weeks and then rate each of their goals on importance, difficulty, commitment, whether they had tried it before (and if so, whether they had succeeded or not), and whether they had the abilities and resources to accomplish the goal.

She asked the other four groups to write down their goals and rate them according to the same items she gave to the first group. She asked Group Three to also write "action commitments" for each of their goals. She had Group Four to write goals, action commitments, and also share them all with a friend. Group Five had to do everything the other groups had to do and also had to send progress reports each week to their friend.

At the end of the study, only 149 of the participants had even completed it. Group One only met 43 percent of their goals, while Group Four met 64 percent of their goals. However, on average Group Five met 76 percent of their goals, almost twice the success of Group One. In other words, it's not only a good idea to write down your goals, but also to share them with a friend who will hold you accountable for meeting them and then regularly report your progress to your friend.

Stick to Your Goals: Stay Motivated and Believe

As Zig Ziglar once said, "People often say that motivation doesn't last. Well, neither does bathing—that's why we recommend it daily." So how do you keep yourself motivated? In addition to writing down your goals, read them daily to remain focused on them. Share them with someone who will hold you accountable. It is also important to make sure you reward and recognize yourself for your accomplishments. Reward yourself for every milestone you make along the way. Decide what your reward is ahead of time so that you'll feel even more motivated to meet each milestone.

If you're willing to stand behind your goals to the point you do all these things, then there's a good chance you'll stick with pursuing them. Staying focused on your goals by thinking about them and reading them every day will help as well. At the end of the day, you're the one who ultimately decides whether you will achieve your goal or not. In fact, consciously or not, we've often decided before we even start whether we are going to meet our goals or not.

Let me tell you about a guy named Bob. He decided ahead of time that he was going to stick with his goal. His decision resulted in a multi-million dollar sales conversation for him. We were working on building a relationship with one of the largest insurance companies in the world. We had been working with this customer for years and only doing transactional business. They would order cameras, printers, toner, cables, computers, and items that were commodities. Bob and I had several conversations regarding strategy on the account each year.

Each year, we would look at the account and the potential and build a strategy to penetrate the account. One year, we decided to spend a significant amount of time working with our manufactures like Hewlett Packard, Cisco, IBM, and EMC to come up with a joint game plan. We asked our executive team to get engaged with the account for sponsorship. We continued to try everything we could and always gave 100 percent.

Each year, we would get a little more from the customer in terms of spend, but nothing compared to what they could do. We made hundreds of calls into the account of the years and had just as many meetings. As it turns out, four year later, the customer signed a multi-million-dollar deal with Bob.

Bob set his sights on his goal, decided to stick with it, and never gave up. He will continue to see the success of his efforts. Sometimes it can be easy to give up and move on, however, if you want to have million dollar sales conversations, you need to make sure you set long-term goals and stick with them.

Let me tell another story about a guy we'll call Ed. You may know someone who's like this. Whenever he would sit in on the weekly sales meetings at his company and the manager would set forth their team sales goals for the week, he would raise an eyebrow. Secretly, they called him "Eyebrow Ed" because the eyebrow raise always meant one thing. He didn't believe the sales team could reach the goal.

So when it came time for each salesperson to write down their own goals, which they told the manager but not each other, his goal was always significantly lower than the goals of his peers. And he almost never met that goal. On one level, you could say that his doubt translated into an inability to perform, and that's certainly true. However, just observing Ed on the sales floor would provide more clues about why he almost never met his sales goal.

He often came in late and took an extended lunch. He usually said he would work late to make up for the missed time, but he never did. When he did converse with a customer, he was usually just shooting the breeze about some random topic rather than looking for a way to help the person or learn more about their needs.

Eventually, he left after it became clear—at least to everyone else, anyway—that he hated his job. As a result of how he felt about his job, he never stuck to his goals. As you can see, there was more than one factor playing a role in why he didn't stick to his goals. Not only was this attitude impacting his ability to succeed, it impacted the ability of the whole team. Ed is the type of person that will have a very short career because he creates poison for the team. He not only doesn't believe it's possible for him and the team to meet their goals, but he also makes it impossible for others because he doesn't care one bit about the goals that have been set by his co-workers and his team.

Let Nothing Stop You

Throughout this chapter, you may have had felt the urge to make excuses for why you haven't met your goals in the past. You may even feel like you had a very good reason for not meeting your goals because you were facing some serious adversity. But no matter what you're facing, you can overcome it, if you have the desire.

In January 2014, I read a news article in *The Guardian* about a man named James Grant. Grant is a doctor in New Zealand who fought off a shark, stitched up his own leg, and then went to the pub to have a beer. Yes, just another day at the office. Grant told the New Zealand newspaper *Stuff* that he had been spearfishing with his friends on weekend when a shark attacked him. Luckily, he had a knife in his hand, so he stabbed the shark. It let go, and he swam to shore, and peeled off his borrowed wetsuit. He saw the bite marks stretching up to five centimeters in length along his leg. He just went to his vehicle and used the first aid kit he kept in there for pig hunts to stitch up the bites. Then he went to a local pub with his friends to have a beer. They kindly gave him a bandage because his blood was dropping all over the floor.

Now all of that is some serious adversity. It's also so bizarre that you just can't make up a story like that. He told the newspaper that as soon as he got the stitches out, he would be right back in the water. Clearly he knew what he wanted, and he wouldn't let anything, even a shark bite, keep him from doing it—or even push back his timeline.

How Adversity Can Help

Wherever there's adversity, there's opportunity as well. You may have heard of Bethany Hamilton, who made news when she also survived a shark attack. She, however, lost her arm in the attack. The 2011 film *Soul Surfer* focused on her story and followed her 2004 autobiography entitled *Soul Surfer: A True Story of Faith,*

Family, and Fighting to Get Back on the Board. Less than a month after the shark bit her, she was back on her surfboard. She taught herself to surf with one arm, initially using a special board until she learned how to adapt her style so she could still enjoy her favorite sport using only the one arm. She's still a professional surfer today, taking first place in several major competitions.

So what's the moral of Bethany's story? Her goal of being a professional surfer was so important to her that she overcame a shark bite and did whatever it took to surf professionally again. She already had at least two first place titles to her name, and she won a lot more after losing her arm. She also used her experience as an opportunity to inspire others to greatness and to share her personal faith in God with others.

You've probably never fought off a shark, but take a moment right now and think about the adversity you have faced. If it kept you from meeting your goals, start thinking about the opportunities you could have enjoyed if you had only seen them—rather than seeing only the adversity itself.

Leveraging Your Goals and Goal Setting

If you haven't already started to do this, get a pen and a notebook and start writing down some ideas about what your goals should be. It helps to initially just get them down on paper so that you can look at them while you think about them. You can also analyze them in the early stages. Ask yourself if they're specific, measurable, achievable, realistic, and time-bound.

Start with a very broad, long-term goal. This should be something you can and want to achieve within the next 10 years. Make sure it is something that can be measured, although the measurements you use will differ depending on what the goal is. Once you have the broad goal, you can begin to "reverse engineer it." That means you'll work backward to determine what you'll need to do to reach the big goal. Each step to the goal will consist of smaller goals or milestones, which are the stepping stones on the way to that big goal. Each one of the milestones you meet will provide you with a little more leverage in achieving your big long-term goal. The more leverage you have, the closer you move toward your million-dollar conversation—that conversation which results in you meeting your long-term goal.

Let's take a look at an example.

Long-term goal: Be CEO of a major corporation

Is this specific? – Yes

Is it measurable? – Yes, with the proper sub-goals

Is it achievable? – If you don't believe it's achievable, then why are you setting this goal? You're only setting yourself up for failure.

Is it relevant? – Obviously if you aren't on a career path which can lead you to become a CEO and have no desire to actually do this, then it isn't relevant.

Is it time-bound? – If you want to do this in 10 years, then yes, this is time-bound.

At this point, it's also good to add two more letters to the acronym, making it SMARTER, with the last two letters standing for evaluate and review. You should be regularly evaluating your goals and reviewing them to make sure that they continue to fit all of the above criteria.

Creating Your Roadmap

So if you're in middle management now, and you want to be CEO, where should you go next to achieve that goal? One of the dangers of being in middle management is remaining near the middle of the pack. You may never stand out from the rest of the middle management, either in a positive or a negative way unless you've set goals to do so. The key to moving up to CEO is to make yourself noticeable to upper management in a positive light. Take the lead and be bold in offering your ideas.

To get an idea of some of the stepping stones you might create on the path to becoming CEO, let's look at the career of Satya Nadella', who was named the third CEO in Microsoft's history in 2014. Here are some of his previous positions:

- Executive Vice-President – Cloud and Enterprise group
- Corporate Vice-President – Business Solutions and Search and Advertising Platform Group
- Vice President – Business Division
- Senior Vice-President of Research and Development – Online Services Division
- President – Server and Tools Division
- CEO - Microsoft

If you want to be CEO of your own company, you should have an idea of how your company is structured. You can then create the stepping stones, which will lead to your goal. Within each of those stepping stones, you'll have conversations which lead to the achievement of one of your sub-goals.

For example, Nadella has many credits to his name despite the fact that he worked behind the scenes at Microsoft for years. He was relatively unknown when he was named to the top spot, but many credit him with transforming the company's culture from one focused on client services to one focused more on the cloud. Every conversation he had during this transformation process took him closer to the million dollar conversation—the one in which he was offered the CEO position.

You could then further break down the steps toward achieving your million dollar conversation into smaller steps, starting with the thousand dollar conversation, then the $10,000 conversation, followed by the $100,000 conversation, and so on. Each of these conversations is the result of a series of action steps you needed to take in order to reach these conversations.

Putting This into Action

Ready to get started? Let's break this down into a step-by-step process to review.

1. **Write down your goals.** This will force you to clarify what you want, giving you a sort of road map to your million dollar conversation. Without clarity, it will be impossible to achieve your goals.

2. **Read your goals every day.** This will keep you motivated because there's nothing like reminding yourself about what lies ahead at the end of the road to keep you moving. The journey can seem long and tiresome while you're on it, but reminding yourself of the progress you have made will help you keep going.

3. **Share your goals with a friend and give them regular progress reports.** Choose a friend who will hold you accountable for making progress and cheer you on as you go. You may even be able to reciprocate so that you can both help each other achieve your goals.

4. **Examine every opportunity that comes your way.** As you achieve each milestone toward your long-term goals, you'll notice that the number of doors that are opened to you tends to increase dramatically. In other words, the more successful you become, the more opportunities others will extend to you. Every time you receive a new opportunity, you should look at it through the lens of your written goals. Is the opportunity something that will help you achieve your goal? Is it something which could, down the road, lead to your million dollar conversation? If not, then it's best to pass on the opportunity and wait for the next one.

5. **Realize that you will face resistance.** If you're willing to give up on your goals when you face resistance, then you probably haven't set the right goals for yourself. The right goals are those you must achieve no matter what—come hell, high water, or shark bite. The right goals are those you need to achieve as much as you need to breathe.

6. **See resistance as yet another opportunity.** Rather than focusing on the resistance, focus on the goal itself. See how the resistance you're facing will open up new paths

of success you might not have even thought of. Resistance may even provide a short cut to bring you closer to that million dollar conversation in a shorter time frame than you previously expected, if you see it as an opportunity, not a wall.

7. **Celebrate your progress along the way.** Sometimes the best motivation is a celebration that reminds you that you are indeed making progress and that you will be able to achieve your goal within the time frame you have set for yourself.

8. **Remind yourself of your goals every single day.** Don't just read them, but visualize them and see yourself sticking with them. If you've set SMART goals, then you will be able to achieve them—but only if you remain focused on those goals and move a little closer to them each and every day.

9. **Create a roadmap of sub-goals or stepping stones.** Each stepping stone should contain action steps—items you must complete in order to achieve each stepping stone, which serves as a marker that measures your progress. Each action step culminates in another major conversation. Each major conversation brings you closer to your million dollar conversation and, ultimately, the achievement of your goal.

10. **Evaluate and review your goals on a regular basis.** This will help you not only remain focused on your goals so that you can keep them in sight, but will also encourage you to check to see if your goals are evolving over time. It isn't uncommon to see small changes in your roadmap as you progress. Your interests and desires can change over time, so you may need to make some small adjustments to your goals. Also, as new opportunities related to your

long-term goal emerge, the action steps in your roadmap could also change a bit, thus evolving the goal-keeping process.

CHAPTER 4

Listening

	Have you ever dealt with anyone who didn't really listen to what you said?
	How did that make you feel?
	Has anyone ever told you that you are/aren't a good listener?
	If so, did you agree with the person? Why or why not?
	What are some things you could do to be a better listener?

President Franklin D. Roosevelt gazed down the long line of guests who were coming into the big White House party. The line had to be half a mile long or so. Working up his brightest smile, the president shook every hand that was offered to him, murmuring to each person, "I murdered my grandmother this morning." Everyone who shook the president's hand smiled and gave standard responses like, "Marvelous," or, "Great to see you."

Finally, he came to Mr. Smith, a dapper-looking man in formal attire and holding a hat in his hand. He reached over and shook Roosevelt's hand, and the president delivered his line again. "I murdered my grandmother this morning." Mr. Smith smiled and said, "She certainly had it coming."

Hearing Versus Listening — What's the Difference?

This story is retold from a story included *in The Wordsworth Book of Urban Legend: Tall Tales for Our Times*, from the *Wordsworth Reference Series*. No one really knows if the story is rooted in urban legend or not, but supposedly, President Roosevelt was testing out a theory another hostess had previously tested. As the story goes, he had heard that those who attend social functions don't pay any attention to the murmured small talk doled out at such events.

Supposedly he heard of a well-known hostess who had tested the theory herself. She smiled when bidding each of her guests good night and said, "It was a terrible thing for you to have come. I do hope you never come again." And of course no one paid attention to what she said.

We could argue that in both of these cases, no one heard what they said, but in reality, they just weren't listening. So what's the difference between hearing and listening? Of course hearing is the (somewhat) physical action that occurs when your eardrums vibrate and sound waves travel through the air, into your ears, and to your brain. Listening is what happens when you actually hear *and comprehend* what the other person is saying.

Two Ears but Just One Tongue

It's pretty easy to say that listening is important. After all, how are you going to fulfill a customer's needs if you don't listen to what they say? Ancient Greek biographer Diogenes Laertius once said, "We have two ears and only one tongue, in order that we may hear more and speak less." Unfortunately though, the numbers show that most people tend to speak more than they listen.

Listening is such an important and difficult skill that one group has done extensive study on it and even holds an annual convention about it. Through years of study, the International Listening Association (ILA) has put together some very interesting statistics about listening.

For example, did you know that, on average, humans listen at only a 25% comprehension rate? That means you probably don't comprehend 75% of what you hear. Now think about how much more often you could end up in a Million Dollar Conversation if you comprehended more of what you heard. The possibilities are endless! The ILA also found that 85% of what we know, we learned through listening. This just goes to show that we have the opportunity to learn even more, simply be listening more carefully. And the more we know, the better we're able to help customers.

Researchers also say we talk at a rate of 125 to 175 words per minute and listen at a rate of 125 to 250 words per minute but think at a rate of 1,000 to 3,000 words per minute. Researchers say the gap between these rates unfortunately creates opportunities for us to become distracted and, thus, fail to listen carefully to what the speaker is saying.

So how can we reduce the distractions and stay focused on what our customers are saying? If you're coming up empty on ideas, you're not alone. The ILA also found that less than 2% of professionals have actually had formal education or training to understand and improve their listening skills and techniques. So, let's do something about this.

Why <u>Active</u> Listening is Important in Sales

American psychiatrist Karl A. Menninger once said, "Listening is a magnetic and strange thing, a creative force. The friends who listen to us are the ones we move toward. When we are listened to, it creates us, makes us unfold and expand." In other words, truly listening to a customer gets them to open up, share more about their life, and give you a foothold in creating a relationship that can lead to bigger and better things. The key to becoming a better listener is listening actively rather than passively. Let me give you an example. Please note there are many important things in this example because it deals with giving a presentation. Believe it or not, you can be a great listener even in situations when it seems like you're supposed to be the one doing the talking.

I was training the team on how to manage a meeting and be a great presenter. I was working with them on how to keep your audience engaged. As we started the meeting, I asked them to role-play as customers and for each to take a different role in a fake organization. All of them had extensive experience presenting to customers, so they knew the dynamics of running a meeting.

I started the meeting by using the whiteboard and having the first slide of my presentation displayed on the opposite wall. The first thing I did was ask the group if they minded if I stood while I presented. This was to get the audience engaged in the meeting, and get them involved. I proceeded to write the agenda on the white board. The agenda was easy, with four main topics: introductions, the goals and priorities of ABC Company, solutions, and questions.

I introduced myself and gave a 30-second commercial on who I was and why they should do business me. I talked about my experience, background, and some relevant customer information that related to their company. I then asked each person in the room to introduce themselves and provide one or two of their main priorities or challenges. As they talked about themselves and their main priorities, I wrote them on the whiteboard.

After everyone in the room was done talking, we had 10 main items on the board. Now I knew exactly how to tailor my presentation to address everyone's main areas of concern. The content of the slides I prepared the day before was not important. The most important thing to do in the room was discuss what was important to them using the slides I had.

It's important to realize that most people are not reading your slides. They are more interested in what you're saying and how you're involving them. It's important to keep each person in the room engaged. Otherwise they will wonder why they are in the meeting in the first place. In addition, they are probably distracted and multitasking while you're presenting. This is a sure sign that you have lost them.

The great thing about doing introductions before giving a presentation is that you can use their name in the meeting and ask them questions as you present. Continue to keep them engaged in the meeting while you are presenting. Your presentations should be interactive and more of a dialogue than just you presenting. If you catch yourself presenting and doing all the talking, you're doing something wrong. The people in the room and in the meeting are going to be your champions as you work on solutions to solve their priorities and objectives. You want each of them to know that they are just as important as anyone else in the room.

Actively listening is the key to being able to build dialogue in the meeting. Listening engages everyone in the meeting on an ongoing basis. If you aren't actively listening to what the members of the meeting are saying, you will never be able to build solutions that support their goals. Having million dollar sales conversations will not happen if you don't engage your listeners.

So to sum it up, there are five main reasons active listening is so important when it comes to maneuvering yourself into Million Dollar Conversations:

1. It makes you a better communicator.
2. It keeps others engaged with you.
3. It helps you avoid misunderstanding what the customer wants or needs.
4. It gets customers to open up and share more about what they want or need.
5. It keeps customers from getting defensive or becoming more defensive if they already were.

6. It enables you to build a relationship, which of course should be your goal every time you speak with a customer—whether or not you believe the customer is about to buy from you or not.

What Active Listening Isn't

You may have heard the phrase "active listening" before, as the phrase tends to be a buzz word in the business community. There are a lot of misconceptions about what this phrase actually means. When Malcolm Gladwell gave a talk on BBC Radio about listening, he told the story of Konrad Kellen during the Vietnam War.

Anyone who has read any of Gladwell's books or articles is aware that he's an excellent storyteller and writer. He's no different or less engaging when he verbally recounted this story on BBC Radio. Gladwell defines active listening as "the ability to hear what someone says and not filter it through your own biases." In other words, actively listening isn't just mimicking back what people say. It's easy to repeat what others say while thinking in the back of your mind that you completely disagree. Active listening also isn't taking what other people say and running it through your own filter in order to decide what to say back to them, or rearranging their phrases so it sounds like you heard them. Active listeners hear the spaces between the words, and grasp the stories that aren't being told by what is being said.

Gladwell's story about Kellen compares him to Leon Goure, the man Gladwell calls his "great nemesis." In the 1960s after being in the U.S. Army for many years and serving in World War II,

Kellen went to work for a think tank for a project known as the Vietnam Motivation and Morale Project. The Pentagon started the project because they didn't know anything about the North Vietnamese. They wanted to understand the way the Vietnamese think so that they would know when they were breaking the will of the North Vietnamese. The U.S. wanted to get them to stop supporting insurgents in South Vietnam.

So Goure took over an old French villa in Vietnam, hired Vietnamese interviewers, and sent them into the countryside to interview captured Vietcong guerillas. He collected 61,000 pages of transcripts that they translated into English. After analyzing those transcripts, Goure came to the conclusion that the North Vietnamese were very close to giving up.

Specifically, Gladwell pointed to an interview with a senior Vietcong captain. When asked if he thought the Vietcong could win the war, he said no. Goure took that to mean that their will was beginning to break because he filtered through his view that the U.S. was the greatest nation in the world and that North Vietnam was just a tiny speck. Kellen, however, kept reading, or listening, to what the captain said. Pages later, he was asked if he thought the U.S. could win the war, and again, he said no.

Kellen took that to mean that the captain wasn't thinking in terms of winning or losing. Gladwell noted, "The second answer profoundly changes the meaning of the first." He said an enemy who's indifferent to the result of a war is "the most dangerous enemy of all." If U.S. military officials had listened to Kellen, the end of the story would have been much different than it actually turned out.

So what can we learn from this story? Filtering what a customer says through your own biases is very dangerous because you not only risk giving them what they don't actually want or need, but you also risk alienating them completely. It's true that we want to contribute things to a conversation, but our contributions should be focused 100 percent on the other person. If you don't look at things from their point of view, you'll probably lose the sale completely.

It goes back again to the 100 percent rule. You take full responsibility for the relationship, which means any answers you give should not shift the focus of the conversation to yourself. The answers should be focused on contributing to a solution for whatever the customer needs, and remember, you should always arrive at the best solution by looking at things through the eyes of your customer rather than your own eyes.

In addition to looking at things from the other person's point of view, active listening also isn't just looking for openings to express yourself so that you can be understood. In his book, *The 7 Habits of Highly Effective People*, author Stephen R. Covey advises people to "seek first to understand" rather than to be understood. "Most people do not listen with the intent to understand; they listen with the intent to reply," he wrote. "They're either speaking or preparing to speak."

Once again, it's about taking 100 percent responsibility for the relationship. Listen closely and carefully to understand what the other person is saying before you prepare your response. After all, your response could be completely different if you base it on all of what the person just said instead of only the first part of it.

Covey goes on to describe five different levels of listening, four of which he says people usually listen at: ignoring, pretending, selective, and attentive. He lists the fifth level as being "empathic listening," which he defines as "listening with the intent to understand." He goes on to say that empathic listening isn't what people call active listening. He describes active listening as just "mimicking what another person says."

I would disagree with this view. Yes, there is a component of repeating back what the other person says. However, truly active listening goes beyond this. It isn't enough to just repeat back what the speaker said. We need to repeat what the person meant.

What Active Listening Is

Author Peter Drucker hit on one of the key elements of active listening when he said, "The most important thing in communication is hearing what isn't said." Taking in a customer's body language will reveal volumes about what they're really saying. It takes you beyond their words and gives you a picture of what they really mean. By noticing the kinds of physical signals the customer is giving off and also his tone of voice, you'll be able to gather some clues about how you might be able to help.

Does the customer look agitated? Is he standing with his arms folded or his stance more open? Does she look confused? Is she fidgeting? Does she look nervous? What about the customer's tone of voice? Is there an edge to it? Is there a smile accompanying the words? It will take some practice, but with a little bit of work, these sorts of questions will become second nature to you, not requiring any thinking on your part. You'll begin to notice these things automatically.

In addition to taking cues from the customer's body language and tone of voice, you should also ask questions. The goal isn't just to learn more about the customer's wants and needs—although that's important—but to also show interest in what the customer is saying. Asking questions gives you an opportunity to be authentic and learn more about the customer. Learning about the customer helps you build a relationship. Ask questions that are not only related to the reason the customer came to see you, but also others that fit naturally into the conversation, depending on where the conversation goes. If you're building a personal relationship, these sorts of questions should naturally work themselves in.

For example:

- How's the new baby?
- How's the construction on the new house going?
- Where are you relocating to / from?
- Where's the new job?
- Where did you go on vacation?
- How was the place you stayed at when you went on vacation?
- Oh, you like to golf? Where do you go golfing?

Questions like these or whatever else falls within the realm of the conversation you're having, is appropriate. The point is that being inquisitive, without sounding like an interrogator about the other person's life can open up an area of commonality upon which you can build a long-term, positive relationship.

As I've said before, active listening is listening to someone—without running their responses through your own biases. Covey hits on this when he describes what he calls "empathic listening," but I would really include this under active listening because it requires you to actively participate in the conversation, going beyond a simple nod of the head or noncommittal-sounding agreement. Empathizing with the customer demonstrates that you either understand what they're going through because you've been in it yourself or that you're at least imagining what it must be like to go through what they're going through.

Interpreting what the customer is saying goes even further beyond empathizing with them. Sometimes customers say one thing but mean another. Sometimes they're using the wrong terminology for what they need or want. If you're listening closely when they describe what they want, you can often decode their true meaning. By listening carefully you're able to identify that what they're describing is different than the thing they actually said they wanted. Only through active listening, interpretation, and asking further questions about the customer's wants will you be able to get to the heart of the problem and provide the best possible solution.

Listen More, Talk Less

So now that you know what active listening is and what it isn't, let's talk about some of the problems that keep us from actively listening. Probably the number one issue is that we simply talk too much. It's natural to want to contribute to the conversation, but if you find yourself waiting for the other person to stop talking so that you can say what you wanted to say, then it's time to check that tongue at the door.

There are several ways talking too much can negatively affect your relationships and your ability to close a sale. Of course the most basic problem is that you won't hear what the customer says. If you don't hear what the person says, then you won't be able to solve their problem. If you have a tendency to interrupt people—even if you think you're helping—you come off as rude and too self-absorbed. Everyone wants to feel as if they're being heard, and if you interrupt them constantly, they'll move on to someone else. No one likes to be in any kind of relationship with someone who constantly interrupts them.

I talked in chapter two about responding rather than reacting. If you aren't listening well enough, you will be far more likely to react than you are to respond. Reacting is simply waiting for your chance to talk. You've spent most of the time while the other person was talking thinking of what you were going to say so that you can react to what you think they said. However, if you listen to everything they say, as Gladwell basically pointed out, what comes later in the conversation has the potential to entirely change the meaning of the first part of the conversation. By listening fully to all of the other person's words, you can think for a moment and then respond to all of it rather than just reacting to the first part of what the other person said. If you don't do this you'll be skipping over the second part entirely because you were thinking about how to react to the first part.

While talking too much may be the most-recognized reason people are poor listeners, it isn't the only reason. President Bill

Clinton once said, "Being president is like running a cemetery; you've got a lot of people under you and nobody's listening."

Of course the dead don't talk back, but their lifelessness gives us some clues about what a poor listener looks like. Let's go through a couple of other bad habits people suffer from by having poor listening skills. Then, I'll give you some tips to break down some of the most common barriers to effective listening.

Listen Slowly

Many people fail to listen slowly enough. They're just too busy, so they insert the proper verbal affirmation, telling the speaker that they have supposedly heard what was said. The response ends up being very flat. The impression the speaker has is that it looks like the lights are on, but nobody's home. In his book *Stress Fractures*, author Chuck Swindoll tells of something he learned from his daughter. She said he wasn't listening slowly enough to what she said because he was just too busy.

Failing to take your time to listen slowly enough to what the other person is saying prevents you from building a long-term relationship with that person. It doesn't take long to realize that someone isn't really hearing what you're saying because they're doing other things. Would you spend a lot of time trying to develop a relationship with someone who was just too busy to spend time with you or even to listen to what you had to say? Of course not because it's a waste of time. There are plenty of other people who will take the time to build a relationship with you.

Not listening slowly enough also keeps you from learning anything, whether it's information about the people you want to build relationships or just new things that interest you, or that you didn't know before. Talk show host Larry King said he reminds himself every morning, "Nothing I say this day will teach me anything. So if I'm going to learn, I must do it by listening." You can't learn anything if you don't take time to build the relationship by truly listening to what the other person says. The International Listening Association (ILA) says 85 percent of what we learn, we learn through listening. If you don't listen, you're certainly missing out on a lot. The ILA also says most people remember only approximately 20 percent of what they hear. Just think how much more you could learn about new contacts if you remembered more of what you heard.

Listen Beyond Their Words

It's also common for people to fail to listen beyond the other person's words. As I've already mentioned, this is an important part of active listening, and here's why. An article published in the *Psychiatry* journal entitled "Nonverbal Communication in Psychotherapy" by Gretchen N. Foley, MD and Julie P. Gentile, MD states that about 60 to 65 percent of interpersonal communication comes through "nonverbal behaviors," many of which are unconscious.

In other words, not only should you be picking up on body language and tone of voice, but you should also look for unconscious gestures or behaviors. These unconscious gestures may provide better insight into what the other person is really thinking if you learn how to interpret them. The person you're speaking with may not even be totally aware of how they feel about the subject they're talking about. But the subconscious always knows. If you listen beyond their words, you may actually be able to help them figure out how they feel. This is something psychologists, therapists, and psychiatrists learn to master in order to help patients deal with problems.

Salespeople must also master this skill if they want to be successful. Think of yourself as the customer's therapist, in a business sort of way. You can't solve their problem effectively if they themselves are not entirely aware of how they feel about the issue. Listen beyond the words they are speaking. Learn to decode the other elements of the conversation and you'll be able to walk them through how they're really thinking and feeling. When we know what our customer's true feelings and intents are, we can help them arrive at the best possible solution for their needs. The customer will not only be surprised at how well you were able to help, but will also remember their encounters with you vividly. They'll see you as someone who not only cares and listens, but understands. They'll keep coming back often to keep the relationship going and will probably also refer others to you.

Maria, a nursery and garden center owner, noticed a new customer and her daughter looking at various plants and pots. She noticed that unlike most customers, the woman didn't pick up the pots or touch the plants. When her daughter attempted to do so the woman brushed her hands off with a handkerchief and gently scolded her. Since most gardeners revel in the touch, smell, and feel of plants and dirt, Maria knew something was off. Rather than say anything directly she picked up two sets of new gardening gloves and handed them to the woman and her daughter. "You have on such a lovely outfit I would hate to see you get it dirty," she said. The woman was visibly moved and put the gloves on. "Thank you," she said. "My daughter and I love plants but we're both so allergic to so many things I was afraid to touch anything." Suddenly the woman's body language made sense.

So, Maria spent time talking with them, walking them through the center and pointing out which plants were most likely to trigger a pollen or other allergy and which ones were not. Because Maria took time to notice what the woman wasn't saying, but her what her body language was telling her, she was able to help her customer solve her problem. She ended up being the garden center the woman selected to work with her landscaper because she felt Maria truly understood her concerns.

When you notice something off or different about a person's body language, you don't have to confront it directly. In fact, it's better not to. By offering the solution she did Maria was able to find out what really concerned the woman.

Breaking Down Common Barriers to Listening

If you can master all aspects of active listening, then you can become an effective listener. Listening effectively means you are able to gather all of the pieces of a conversation and use them to build a complete picture of what the customer wants and needs. J.C. Penney founder James Cash Penney once said, "The art of effective listening is essential to clear communication, and clear communication is necessary to management success."

Of course effective listening is also essential to success in sales and relationships in general. In order to become a more effective listener, however, you must be able to identify the barriers you deal with—both the personal habits we've already covered and the outside barriers we're about to discuss. Then you must take the time to tackle each of these barriers.

You may think you're actually pretty good listening. Most people think they're better at it than they actually are, but there are some warnings signs to consider. *Psychology Today* has a listening skills test which shows us some warning signs to watch out for. Ask yourself these questions:

- Do you do other things and/or daydream while listening to someone talk?
- Do you interrupt people?
- Do you wait anxiously for your turn to speak in the conversation?
- Do you fidget while other people talk?
- Do you make faces when you don't like what other people are saying?
- Do you correct people when they mispronounce a word?

These are just a few of the warning signs you should look for when it comes to listening. If you do all or some of these things, then you probably aren't as good of a listener as you think you are. Be honest with yourself. It's also a good idea to ask people who know you well for some help. Ask them if you have any "tells." Those who know you well will probably be able to share one or two things you tend to do when you aren't really listening to what they're saying. Knowing these bad habits will make it easier for you to tackle them.

Unfortunately there's more than just conquering bad habits when it comes to being an effective listener. Aside from the personal habits you may have to deal with, there are also many external reasons you may have trouble listening. If you find your mind wandering during a conversation, take a moment to consider these external barriers. Look for a solution so that you can focus entirely on what the other person is saying. If necessary and possible, move the conversation to a different location to eliminate distractions. If you have a short attention span, practice with friends on lengthening it.

There are many reasons why you may not be able to focus on what a person is saying. For example, your environment plays a big role in whether you can listen effectively. Noises are a common distraction, and there are probably many times you'll have to find a solution to this. Meeting with a client in a noisy restaurant may seem like a good idea at first because the food is excellent and the atmosphere is relaxed and fun, but it's much better to choose a place you know will be quiet in order to minimize distractions. Or, you can enjoy the atmosphere, but save business talk for the drive back to the office, or another time. You may consider taking some time to scout out good places to meet with clients ahead of time. Consider the time of day when scouting and deciding where to meet. A place that might be extremely busy at one time of the day may be quiet at another.

If you're working in a building where there are renovations going on, then move to another part of the building or step outside and enjoy the fresh air while you talk. If other people are talking loudly and distracting you, then move away from them. Author Stephen King spoke about this problem, although he was speaking more metaphorically about his state of mind when he said, "No, it's not a very good story—its author was too busy listening to other voices to listen as closely as he should have to the one coming from inside."

Believe it or not, even the lighting in the room or the general environment can have a big impact on how well you are able to listen to someone speak. A room that's too dark, chairs or couches that are too soft, and an office with the temperatures too warm can make it difficult to stay awake enough to fully comprehend what the other person is saying. We can also easily become distracted if the room is too hot or too cold. We become overly focused on how uncomfortable we are rather than what the other person is saying. Make adjustments as needed to ensure that both you and the client are comfortable. After all, if the client isn't comfortable in the environment, he or she probably won't be able to listen effectively to you either. Standing in an aisle or parking lot or on a hard floor can be very hard on some people. Their backs, legs, and feet may hurt. Watch to see if they shuffle around or sway. This is their body telling you, and them, that they're uncomfortable. If you must speak with someone for more than 5 or 10 minutes, seek out a quiet place to sit down. Have your showroom or business place benches or comfortable seating nooks around so this is easy to do.

Sometimes we have personal or mental issues that are distracting us. The loss of a loved one can weigh on our minds, as can dealing with a chronic pain issue or a broken arm or leg. These are the sorts of issues you must come up to a solution for on your own because the same solution won't work for everyone.

We also may have some preconceived notions about a customer that we need to move past. These notions often stem from personal experiences, although stereotypes can also be a big factor here. If we think we know what the other person is going to say because the way they dress suggests they won't spend money with us, then we won't listen nearly as closely to what they say as we might to someone who is dressed more nicely. I once heard about a doctor who was a big do-it-yourself home repair person. One weekend while laying a brick walkway in his backyard he went out to grab a sandwich. He happened to stop at a restaurant next to a Mercedes-Benz dealer. He ate lunch, then went into the car dealership in his work boots, torn jeans and t-shirt to ask about buying a car. All but one salesman ignored him or shrugged him off. That one salesman spent almost an hour explaining the different makes and models. The doctor returned the next day in a suit and tie with a handful of business cards. He was swarmed with salespeople, but ignored them all. He bought a top-of-the-line Mercedes from the salesman the day before who had looked past his dirty hands and clothes to answer his questions and strike up a conversation and a relationship with him.

The goal should always be building a relationship with the person, which means that our ideas about whether the person will spend money with us or not shouldn't even be a consideration. How a person looks, whether poor or wealthy, shouldn't be a factor in how we treat the person or how well we listen to them. If you find yourself with preconceived notions about a customer, banish them from your mind immediately. Get rid of them before you approach the client. If they surface the moment you see them for the first time, make sure you banish the thoughts entirely before approaching the person. If they pop up during a conversation, squash them like a bug by refocusing the conversation on good things about the client.

Some people are nervous when talking to strangers or salespeople. They just aren't comfortable. They may fidget because they're late for a meeting and don't know how to break away from the conversation. They may need to use the restroom. They may feel badly for taking up your time because they don't have the money to buy right then and there. If the person is doing something distracting during the conversation, you may find it hard to focus. If there are children with the person, they may be more focused on the child than on you. If the other person is fidgeting or doing something that distracts you, then you'll have to find a way to tune that out or find a way to eliminate the distraction. With a child, you may offer them a toy or something to drink. Eliminating distractions of all kinds is a skill you must hone over time because it doesn't come overnight. The same technique for various distractions may not necessarily work for everyone.

Another barrier related to distractions is whether what the other person is doing seems to contradict with what he or she is saying. It can be easy to misinterpret the connection between the body language and the words. You may give too much emphasis to the wrong part of the conversation. Once again, this is a skill you must hone over time. You must also be able to adapt because there are many different communication styles. In order to decide how much emphasis to give to each part of the conversation, you'll have to get to know the other person better. Card dealers have a word for body language that betrays a person's true feelings. It's called "a tell." It can be something like a person licking their lips when they're excited, or rubbing their nose when they're bluffing or lying. Some people will say "yes," while nodding "no."

The head nod is more likely to be the true response. Learning a person's tells and other character traits will factor into every conversation you have with them. Just don't be too quick to judge if you run across someone with a lot of common tells. Take extra time getting to know them so that you can learn which parts of the conversation should receive more emphasis. This will enable you to better decode all of your conversations with this person.

Practicing Active Listening

So how can we move beyond these barriers and personal habits to hone our active listening skills? This is indeed something that will take practice. I would advise you not to try to tackle every one of the problems we have discussed all at the same time. Ask someone who knows you well to help you figure out which of the issues is the most problematic for you. Then choose just one or two to work on at a time. It helps to check in regularly with the person you have chosen to help you. Ask them to hold you accountable for making progress and to help you keep track of where you are on your journey to become a better listener.

Putting This Into Action

1. **Avoid filtering what the other person said through your own biases.**
2. If you find your internal voice starting to weigh too heavily on the other person's words, refocus your attention and look at it from their point of view.
3. **Actively take part in conversations.** Don't just rephrase what the other person has said but also taking in tone and body language and asking questions to show interest and

better understand the other person's point of view and problem. Empathize if it's appropriate.

4. **Listen more than you talk.** Allow the other person's words to fully breathe so that you can respond rather than react to everything they have just said.

5. **Stop what you're doing and listen slowly.** You'll hear everything clearly and can take in cues other than the words that are actually being said. This also shows respect for the customer. Never, ever answer your cell phone in the middle of a conversation.

6. **Identify your bad listening habits and external listening barriers and then work on eliminating them.** Role-play and do exercises to banish bad habits and look for practical solutions to external listening barriers.

CHAPTER 5

Encouragement

Encouragement can be as simple as a pat on the back or a sincere "thank you" for doing a good job that day. It could also be a reminder to the person how great he or she is and how much you appreciate them being part of your team.

Following is a story about a colleague that I think demonstrates this. Janice, a new sales associate for a wedding planner, had a discouraging month in which she didn't make one sale. She was considering quitting, thinking she wasn't as good at sales as she thought. She explained her frustrations to the shop owner. The owner held a pot luck luncheon the next Friday. While everyone was eating, laughing and having a good time she had each of the other salespeople share a story about their biggest failure, and then their biggest success with the group. Janice quickly learned that she wasn't the only one who'd gone through tough times. The upside was the encouragement she got from her co-workers when she shared her struggles with the group. Each of them offered advice and tips, and shared with her what they thought her strongest skills were. Within a few weeks Janice had made her first sale and was feeling more positive about her future there.

When it comes to building relationships, encouragement is an important part of the equation. Encouragement is also essential in all aspects of the sales process, whether it involves encouraging yourself after you took a hit, encouraging your customer or contacts, or encouraging your sales staff or coworkers. So what exactly does encouragement look like? Of course it depends on the situation, but there is a general guideline to keep in mind when you're looking for ways to encourage anyone.

Steven R. Covey, author of *The 7 Habits of Highly Effective People*, said, "Treat a man as he is and he will remain as he is. Treat a man as he can and should be and he will become as he can and should be."

So essentially, encouragement should involve treating the person the way he or she can and should be. If it's a potential customer or contact, there can be a broad range of areas in which you can encourage the person. Maybe the customer needs encouragement to uncover a talent hidden behind a desire to be able to do something, like play the piano or golf.

Perhaps the customer needs encouragement in an area of life he or she has allowed you into. After all, building a relationship with someone involves many steps, and you can find opportunities to encourage a contact at many different levels within the relationship. Early in the relationship, you should even encourage the contact to trust in your ability to help them. You do this through active listening and genuinely demonstrating you're there to help them, not just to sell to them. You should also encourage new contacts to get to know you and to share details about their lives and work so that you are better able to help them.

There will be times when you need encouragement and there's no one around to encourage you. You'll need to learn to encourage yourself. Encouraging yourself can take several different forms. This is something personal that only you can decide what works. One essential part of encouraging yourself is rewarding yourself for progress made toward your goals. We touched on this in chapter 3. You may also find that celebrating when you have a big win can be a form of encouragement. When you finally reach that million dollar conversation, reward yourself and prepare for the next step. Remind yourself you're going to go above and beyond where you ever thought you could go.

Sales slumps happen to the best salespeople. To break a sales slump, listen to motivational tapes or post inspirational quotes where you will see them on a regular basis. This type of encouragement should take place on a daily basis, even if you're not in a slump. It can actually help lessen the severity of a slump or cut down on how often you experience a sales slump. If you get into a slump, change your routine. Do something different. Take another approach. If you're already down it can't get worse so take a few risks. Something is bound to reset and get you rolling again. Remind yourself slumps happen. It's as much a part of the sales process as summer and winter are parts of the seasons.

Why Encouragement is Important

You probably already have a general idea about why encouragement is important. Understanding the concrete reasons for encouragement goes a long way toward helping you diagnose a particular relationship. It also helps you determine what kind of encouragement would be helpful in a given situation. Of course, encouragement is needed in any sales environment. No one can be successful 100 percent of the time, but the faster you recover from a slump, the higher your percentages of successes will go. By encouraging yourself and your sales team a bit every day, you'll see recovery much more quickly than if you wait for a serious slump before beginning to roll out encouragement.

Encouragement also helps you and your sales team practice turning negative self-talk to positive self-talk. Psychologists estimate that about 70 to 80 percent of self-talk is negative. With all of that negative self-talk already ingrained in our brains, it's no wonder we get into sales slumps that seem to last forever. The more positive your self-talk is, the easier it will be to recover when you take a hit. You'll also shorten the length of time your slump lasts.

Encouraging customers is also important. Encouraging customers enables you to help them develop skills they either didn't know they had or wished they had. Encouraging skill development is a great way to build up trust and a relationship. When you encourage and support a customer in their struggles you give back to the other person as you take 100 percent responsibility for the relationship. By encouraging a customer or contact to develop a skill, or take a risk, or preserve with a decision, you may also be indirectly encouraging them toward what could end up being a sale or even eventually a million dollar conversation.

Encouragement for customers also helps drive trust within your relationship. People are naturally cautious when it comes to meeting new people and allowing them into their lives. This is especially true with salespeople. Many customers don't start out offering a lot of information about themselves, but you can find ways to coax it out of them with a little encouragement as well as sharing your own information in appropriate ways and times. This will not only enable you to serve them better by finding the best possible solution because you know about their situation, but also shows that you really do have the skills necessary to help them.

Encouraging Customers

Let's start by talking about encouraging your customers. Encouragement is an important part of every relationship, whether personal or professional. It not only shows the other person that you care about them and care about how well they perform on their goals, but it also demonstrates that you know them well enough to speak about their problems. Offering encouragement enables you to support your contacts when they have issues by helping them find the best solution possible.

Sometimes you may not even be dealing with a problem at all. In these cases, you might simply have an opportunity to advance a relationship by just making people feel good about themselves. Your encouragement may give them the courage to explore new things or discover hidden talents. After all, sometimes people just need encouragement, whether it's because they're going through a difficult time or they're unsure of where they're going next.

Harper Lee, author of the classic novel *To Kill a Mockingbird*, expressed her thoughts about encouragement after she wrote the book. According to a profile of the book from the National Endowment for the Arts, at one point, Lee had become so discouraged with her manuscript that she actually threw it out the window and into the snow,

"I never expected any sort of success with 'Mockingbird,'" she said. "... I was hoping for a quick and merciful death at the hands of the reviewers, but, at the same time, I sort of hoped someone would like it enough to give me encouragement."

And what a great deal of encouragement Harper got. She won the Pulitzer Prize for the 1960 novel, which her editors initially warned might only sell a few thousand copies. The book spent at least 41 weeks on the bestseller list and won several other awards as well. Lee herself also received several honors, including the Presidential Medal of Freedom, which President George W. Bush presented to her in 2007. The University of Notre Dame also awarded her an honorary doctorate in 2006.

Case Study—One of the Best Salespeople of All Time: Erica vanderLinde Feidner

Inc.com and CBS Moneywatch both put together lists of the best salespeople of all time. Erica vanderLinde Feidner landed on both lists, essentially because she was such an excellent encourager of salespeople. Before she became the owner of PianoMatchmaker.

com, she was Steinway & Sons' top salesperson around the globe for eight years in a row. She moved more than $41 million worth of pianos priced between $2,000 and $152,000.

Feidner was exceptional at diagnosing what type of customer she was working with and adapting her sales approach to match each customer. Some customers who considered buying pianos were new to music. They were hesitant to buy an instrument because of all the time it would take to learn to play the piano. Experienced piano players see pianos as very personal items they will use for hours on end every single day and don't hesitate to invest. Of course, it's obvious that these two types of customers are worlds apart. There is a whole host of customers who fall somewhere in between those two extremes.

According to the report from CBS Moneywatch, Feidner utilized her teaching skills to work with customers who were considering learning how to play. She worked with them for an hour, giving them a basic lesson so that they could be playing a song on the piano by the time the impromptu lesson was over. For experienced players, she considered every piano's personality and focused on matching the perfect piano with the perfect person. In considering a piano's personality, she thought about the age of the instrument, how to take care of it, the materials it is made from and, most importantly, how it sounded.

In a 1999 article in *The New Yorker*, one of Feidner's customers, journalist James B. Stewart, said many customers saw her as "a force of nature." He said she didn't pressure clients, but rather that after meeting her, many soon find themselves in the grip of musical ambitions they never knew they harbored." In other words, she encouraged customers to develop their piano-playing skills.

Show Customers Why They Should Buy from You

In addition to encouraging contacts about their own skills, you should also provide encouragement about your own skills and expertise. After all, customers who don't believe you can help them won't even allow you the opportunity to try. Part of the process of getting to know new people should involve introducing yourself and explaining why you're qualified to help them.

Author Stephen Schiffman, in his book *The 25 Sales Habits of Highly Effective Salespeople*, listed number 17 as, "Sell yourself."

"Give yourself appropriate credit," he wrote. "Talk about yourself—but be humble (No, the two aren't mutually exclusive.) Convey success, confidence, and flexibility. Highlight past successes, but don't try to one-up the prospect. Try to exhibit the characteristics of a person who makes things happen."

By following his advice, you'll be encouraging the customer to see you as the person who can help him.

Show; don't tell people your expertise. When you're talking with people, adjust your vocabulary and skills up or down so you make the person comfortable. George, a saleperson for a large hardware store met a customer in the aisle who was looking for "metal circle thingies." He had no idea what she was talking about, so he engaged her in a conversation. "Tell me again what you're going to do with these metal circles," he said. The woman, a crafter, pulled out a page from a magazine. On it was a photo of several mason jars, the kind used for canning food. Each jar was secured to a wooden board by a metal strip called a plumber's strap—used for suspending pipes from ceilings.

"Oh," he said. "Those are plumber's straps." He explained how the straps were normally used. He then praised the project she showed him before suggesting two or three other devices that could also be used for what she wanted to do. He didn't just answer her question; he offered alternatives and additional solutions. Because he was, in her eyes, so knowledgeable about what hardware was available she began to routinely seek him out and to refer her friends to him as well when she had a craft or do-it-yourself project.

Encouraging Yourself

Encouraging yourself after you've taken a hit can be one of the most difficult parts of sales. Maybe you somehow missed out on a deal you were sure was a slam dunk. Maybe somehow the customer you spent hours and hours working with suddenly withdrew or disappeared. Maybe you've just been in a slump and haven't been able to close a deal in a while. Whatever is going on, you've got to find the encouragement necessary to move past it—and shorten your down time to as little time as possible.

In a recent interview with BusinessInsider.com, real estate guru and *Shark Tank* investor Barbara Corcoran said she became a successful sales broker only because she was "great at taking a hit and taking rejection." She sees the same thing in the brokers who work for her now as well.

"My top salespeople at the Corcoran Group were earning $7 to $8 million a year, when my average income for a typical salesperson was $48 or $50,000," Corcoran told *Business Insider* CEO and Editor-in-Chief Henry Blodget. Corcoran explained how they did it in a video interview posted on the site. "And I'm telling you, it didn't come down to contacts. It didn't come down even to how hard they work. My worst workers very often worked the hardest. It came down to something to prove in getting back up."

So how do you recover when you take a hit? It's all about encouragement, and successful salespeople find ways to keep themselves encouraged so that when they do take a hit, they're not down for very long. Encouragement should be a daily practice.

Encouragement: As Important as Bathing

Schiffman's 19th habit is "Sell yourself on yourself." Some of his suggestions for regular encouragement include avoiding the radio while on your morning commute and listening to motivational audio instead. This is good advice, particularly if you tend to listen to news stations. The news is filled with negative stories about bad things happening all the time. Listening to a series of negative stories isn't a great way to start the day, particularly if you want to stay encouraged. By simply changing what you listen to, you set a much brighter and better tone for the day.

He also suggests setting specific goals and rewards for meeting those goals. We talked about this in chapter three, and the big reason for doing this is because it keeps you encouraged. Another thing you can do is ask for positive reinforcement from others. Leave yourself positive notes in your car, around your desk and on your bathroom mirror. I know salespeople who keep motivational cards in their wallets so they see an affirmation each time they pull out their credit card or buy something. Others will write themselves positive letters or cards at the beginning of the month. They then have their spouse or a friend mail them for them at undisclosed times so they come as a welcome surprise throughout the month. I like to recommend pairing up with a colleague and taking turns leaving each other positive notes and bits of positive reinforcement. Schiffman also suggests going outside for a while to put things into perspective. You'll be surprised what a nice walk in the park on a beautiful day will do for your mood.

Another way to work on encouraging yourself and staying encouraged is to change the way you look at things. Some may have heard the story of the two shoe salesmen, but for those who haven't, I'm going to tell it here. One of the salesmen had a very encouraging way to look at things, but the other had a very discouraging way. An article from *Forbes* contributor Ron Ashkenas in April 2011 retells the story.

A company sent two show salesmen to an African village that was very far out from anything resembling civilization. When they arrived, both were shocked to see that not a single person in the village wore shoes. Sam saw an opportunity, while Bob saw nothing but a wasted trip. Sam wrote back to the company saying, "No one here wears shoes; send inventory!" But Bob wrote back, "No one here wears shoes; will return home shortly."

See what a difference it makes to change the way you look at a situation? Instead of focusing on all of the negatives, whether they're about the company you work for, the client you're trying to help, or even that headache that's been bothering you for an hour, look at the positives. Sure, your company might be understaffed, but that means more sales—and more commission—for you, but only if you work hard enough. Maybe the client you're trying to help is especially difficult, but the reason he or she is difficult is because he or she keeps changing his mind to more and more expensive items. And if you start refocusing your attention on all these positive things, before you know it, that headache will just disappear.

And the need for encouragement doesn't ever stop, no matter how successful you become. Award-winning author Joyce Carol Oates said, "Honorary degrees and lifetime achievement awards are very encouraging. I know that it might sound strange that a writer who has published many books still needs encouragement, but this is true."

If you've had a long string of wins and suddenly find yourself in a slump, remind yourself of past successes. If you've won any awards, look over the plaques and remind yourself of the salesperson you still are. If you won any honors of any kind, think about what you did to win them and turn your attention toward repeating those successes.

A journalist I met once told me about her "Fan club folder." It didn't happen much, but every month she would get from two to three letters from her readers talking about how much they loved a story she had written, or thanking her for covering their special event, or sending her photos of something that had happened in their lives because of something she had done. Whenever she hit a slump or received a lot of criticism for tackling tough, unpopular stories she would sit down with her fan club folder and read through the dozens and dozens of letters she had collected over the years. It didn't always eliminate the pain, but it did put things in perspective.

Encouraging Your Sales Staff

One of the most controversial things in schools and sports programs today is the practice of giving everyone a trophy for just showing up. While that may make a middle-schooler or kindergartener feel good, it's not the best way to motivate a sales-force. Good salespeople, by their very nature, are competitive. And competitive people tend to be easily excited and easily depressed. It makes managing a sales force a real challenge. You need to find a balance between pushing them and cheering them on as they push themselves.

If you're a sales manager, then you're more than just a manager. You're also a mentor, coach, and advocate to your sales teams. In most cases, you've seen a lot more business and a lot more ups and downs than they have. They look to your experience, suggestions, tips, and even your stories about your own glory days. Sometimes the best encouragement comes from someone you view as a mentor, so as a manager, it is your place to fulfill this need for your teams in a way that fits both your style and personality and theirs.

It's pretty common for sales managers to set up competitions to push their salespeople above and beyond where they thought they could go. Just remember that a little competition is good, particularly because it allows you to hand out awards, which are a source of encouragement themselves. Six-time Emmy and

Golden Globe winner Alan Alda once said, "Awards can give you a tremendous amount of encouragement to keep getting better, no matter how young or old you are."

But while those same awards can be extremely encouraging to those who win them, it can be discouraging for team members who never win. As a result, you should always mentor your salespeople. For those who don't win awards but who have passion, find another way to encourage them. Mentor and coach them into success—until they are the ones who have their days in the award spotlight.

Sad Sammy was the youngest salesperson on a 12-member newspaper ad sales team. He got the nickname "sad Sammy" not because he was sad, but because he never had a frown on his face or a bad thing to say about anything or anyone. He was a raging optimist who genuinely enjoyed his job. That was odd because sad Sammy had the worst sales record of the entire department. When his manager looked at his sales calls record he was shocked. Sammy may have had the lowest number of sales, but his ability to cold call and get appointments was higher than the whole department put together. Sammy excelled at the thing that everyone hated—getting appointments. But he was horrible at closing the sale once he gave his presentation.

His manager pulled Sammy back into the office and mentored him on how to close a sale while at the same time he created an award for "most appointments set" so he could reward Sammy for the thing he did better than anyone. He also had every other sales person spend a day shadowing Sammy when he made cold calls, and he had Sammy go along and shadow the top salespeople to learn how to close. It took time but eventually the entire sales force was making more appointments and Sammy was making more sales. Mentoring can work both ways. Don't get locked into a "one up" and "one down" mentality where someone has to always have all the answers. Make sure your staff shares the wealth and the mentoring, learning *and* teaching.

Take Your Whole Sales Team with You into Success

Great sales managers should not only want success for themselves, but also success for their entire teams. They should want to take their entire teams with them on the ride to success. A great example this is David Novak's training program, which he put into his book entitled *Taking People with You*. He started teaching his training program to employees at Yum! Brands when he was CEO. He has several pieces of advice for motivating and inspiring teams.

One of the things he talks about is listening to your team members. It's pretty common to hold focus groups with your company's targeted demographic group to determine if there is a want and a need for your product and service. But Novak essentially says to do the same thing with your team members. As them what is and isn't working. This motivates them to do their best.

He also says that you should be telling your employees what the reality is and also giving them hope. Define the reality by telling them both the good and the bad and then show them where they have the potential to be. Novak uses a quote from Napoleon Bonaparte, who said, "A leader is a dealer in hope." So deal out some hope to inspire your sales team by showing them their potential as well as stating the reality.

Novak also recommends that you make it possible for salespeople to come up with solutions on their own, and he's certainly right. Former President Dwight D. Eisenhower picked up on this when he said, "Motivation is the art of getting people to do what you want them to do because they want to do it."

How often have you been told to do something and you didn't do it because you didn't understand why you should do it or otherwise just thought it was a dumb idea? According to Novak, the key is get your salespeople to explore, discover, and take ownership in their jobs or careers.

"Don't you feel the biggest sense of ownership over ideas, actions, or conclusions you've come to on your own, as opposed to something you've been told to do?" Novak wrote. "The fact is, 'I said it, so do it' or 'I did it, so you do it' just doesn't cut it for motivating and inspiring the very people you need to take with you to the top."

You may have known people who have a knack for planting the seed of an idea in their boss' head and then making him think it was his idea—just so he would do it. This same principle holds true for your sales team. The only difference is you're serving as a mentor who is guiding them rather than an employee who just wants to control the boss. As they explore and discover, a talented manager can give them a nudge or two along the way so that they end up at the right place in the end.

Case Study—What Not to Do: John H. Patterson of National Cash Register

While Novak's training program is fairly well known today, another training program lives on in infamy because the man who created it—John H. Patterson—is now considered to be one of the worst bosses of all time. In honor of National Boss Day in October 2010, *Time* magazine put together a list of the top 10 worst bosses of all time. CNBC also compiled a list of the worst bosses, and once again, Patterson was on it. In addition to being a terrible boss, the once head of National Cash Register (now NCR Corporation) is also known for his primer on sales training. If you want to know what not to do, this guy pretty much covers all the bases.

Patterson's managerial style basically involved tearing people down constantly. He aimed to break his workers' self-esteem by firing them so that he could rehire them later. He forced all of his employees to be weighed and measured every six months (this can be highly discouraging for many people, particularly those trying to lose weight). *PC Magazine* claims he fired people for outlandish things like not being able to properly ride a horse.

The *Wikipedia* entry on Patterson claims that he even fired people for being unable to explain why the flags were flying on a particular day. In addition, it suggests that working for Patterson became the equivalent for earning an MBA degree during his day because of how many prominent businessmen he trained and then fired. The tabloids of his day were also rife with stories of abusiveness in his personal life, so it's unclear whether any of these claims are a bit exaggerated, but you get the idea. He wasn't the best of bosses by anyone's estimates.

Discouragement may seem like a good way to motivate employees to do better, but really all you're doing is motivating them to leave your company. That not only creates a bad name for you, but it also means you waste your time training a bunch of people who can't stand to work with you and just end up leaving even if you taught them a lot. It's not the wisest of training methods because you never know if you're teaching your future competitor, or maybe even your future boss.

Aside from his sales primer and notoriety within the sales industry, Patterson also became famous for firing Thomas Watson, who later headed up IBM, which later became a serious competitor for NCR. Perhaps the most appalling thing about the way he fired Watson was that he supposedly put Watson's desk out on the front lawn for him to find when he went back to the office. If that's not motivation to take a job somewhere else and outperform your boss in a big way, then I don't know what is.

Make it Look Easy to Fix Mistakes

So if that's what not to do, then how should you actually encourage your sales team? Author Jeffrey Gitomer gave talks for Dale Carnegie Training about Carnegie's various principles. One of the principles that apply in this case is number 29, which is "Use Encouragement." More specifically, Gitomer explains that a good manager will help a struggling team member by not only instructing them about what they're doing wrong, but also showing them how to fix it. In fact, he said you should do this by making the fault seem like it's something very easy to correct.

So while criticism is important when it comes to mentoring and teaching, it should be done in the spirit of encouragement. Whenever you see progress, be sure to praise your team members. Encourage them both as individuals and as an entire team—just as you would critique and teach a colleague. Teaching should always be carried out in a positive light. Former *New York Times* executive editor Jill Abramson was exactly right when she observed, "In one's relationship with both dogs and with a newsroom, a generous amount of praise and encouragement goes much better than criticism."

And the same goes with any sales environment as well. Encouragement in every direction goes a long way toward drawing people into the million-dollar conversation you are seeking.

One of the things George hated most about five o'clock was that his sales staff would return from their appointments complaining about all the missed sales, bad clients, bad appointments, or lack of money they'd had or made that day. He didn't like the fact that when they all left at 5:30 it was often on a negative note. Rather than chastise them about their attitudes he simply had each salesperson write down on a huge white board in the salesroom three good things that happened to them each day. They couldn't leave until they had come up with three positive things they'd experienced or learned every day. No one was allowed to write the same thing, which meant people hurried to come up with something and write it down before someone else did. George's other rule was that no one could go home until everyone had written down their three things. As a result, each salesperson quickly learned to pump their co-workers for positive details about their day so they could leave work on time. They didn't have time to complain about the bad events. They were too focused on finding the good ones. Over time, George began to see the salespeople mentoring, encouraging and coaching each other.

Putting Encouragement into Action

Encouraging others does take time, but it is time that's well worth it. Some people find that encouraging others comes easy to them, while others may need a little more practice. Think over your conversations from today or even the last week. How often did encouraging words come out of your mouth? Now think about how often you said discouraging words and consider how you could have changed them around. Going forward, look for opportunities to encourage others, no matter what kind of relationship you have with them or where you are in the relationship.

If the words seem foreign and strange coming out of your mouth, then you'll need to practice with a partner you trust. Try some role-playing to get used to the idea of encouraging others. Even if you don't feel like you have a particularly hard time encouraging others, you can still improve by training your mind to be constantly on the lookout for places where you could insert some encouraging words.

For Customers

1. **Begin asking questions to get to know the customer.** Start by asking questions about things you've observed about the person, whether it's a question about how old their toddler is or about what type of product they are looking for. From there, you can strike up a conversation

and get to know the customer. The better you get to know the person, the easier it will be for you to help them when it comes time to do so.

2. **Find out where they need encouragement.** This should preferably be in the area of your expertise, but it may also be on a related issue or even something else entirely. Remember, you're aiming for a personal relationship that also happens to be a business one.

3. **Build up your relationship by providing encouragement along the way.** This step is one that will take some time. Relationships aren't built overnight, and encouragement should be a constant process. Always be on the lookout for common interests upon which to build and develop your relationships.

For yourself

1. **Seek advice from more experienced salespeople.** No matter what skill you're trying to improve it will take practice, and others who are more experienced than you will be able to share some pointers to help you improve your skill. The reason seeking help from others is the first step in encouraging yourself is because it provides a base for you to start from. After you have some ideas about what you can do to improve, you'll have something concrete to work toward. Sometimes simply knowing what to do to get better is encouragement enough, at least temporarily.

2. **Ask for their success stories.** Everyone has stories about their successes, and sometimes it helps to hear what someone else did to win their million dollar conversation.

Just hearing about how they did it will encourage you to see that it can indeed be done and give you some ideas about how to do it for yourself.

3. **Remind yourself of your past successes.** Don't forget that you have your own success stories. Draw upon your past successes to remind yourself that you are indeed able to win—whatever that looks like in your life at the current moment. Don't dwell on the past, however, as this can hold you back. Think about your past successes just enough to remind yourself that you're able to succeed in the future because you have in the past. Also use your past successes to remind yourself of which techniques or methods work for you.

4. **Encourage yourself daily.** This can take different forms for different people, but everyone needs to keep themselves encouraged every single day. You may find that listening to motivational tapes works great for you, particularly if you have a long commute or another time during the day when it is convenient to do so. Other ideas include posting inspirational quotes where you will see them constantly and rewarding yourself when you achieve a goal. Use any combination of these suggestions and others you come up with to keep your motivation at the highest level possible.

5. **When you do take a tumble, get right back up.** Everyone takes a hit at different times, so you can expect things to go wrong sometimes. But if you've taken time each day to encourage yourself, then you won't waste a lot of time feeling sorry for yourself and dwelling on what went wrong. Encouragement will help you recover from a hit faster than the average salesperson who doesn't take the time for self-encouragement each day.

For Your Sales Team

1. **Hold regular team building sessions to foster a sense of connectedness.** While it's true that each salesperson must be able to perform individually, it's also important to remember that you're part of a team. No one likes to feel like they're out there all alone, so make sure that you're regularly reminding your team members that they're part of a bigger force and that there are others to help them out when they need it.

2. **Watch for inspirational stories/handouts you can provide to employees.** Just because you aren't having a sales or team building meeting, it doesn't mean that you can't provide some encouragement. Keep a sharp lookout for inspirational items you can hand out to your staff. If you send out regular memos or emails, include an inspirational segment with it. If you email the memo, this can be as simple as providing a link to an inspirational article or video you found on the web.

3. **Keep morale up through regular competitions and rewards.** A certain amount of competition is healthy, and it's good to foster this kind of competition. In addition to offering rewards for the top salespeople each week or month, you should also offer rewards for team members who exceed their own goals and achieve a new personal best. This will help coax them out of the shell and give them some recognition for the progress they make. It can be discouraging to always lose because you're up against someone with 20 years' more experience. But when you're only competing with yourself, it becomes much easier to win. When you're beating your "personal best," you're just beating something you've already personally done—not

something someone else has done. When you're competing with yourself, the taste of victory is often even sweeter than when you're competing with someone who has so much more experience than you that it's impossible for you to win.

4. **Provide encouragement when employees seem to be in a rut.** Competitions are good, but for those who constantly lose, they can be a real discouragement. Also remember that every employee will have a slump at some point. Both of these types of situations are your opportunities to come alongside them and provide the encouragement and guidance they need to recover. Ask them what's wrong and then offer some pointers to help them get it right the next time. Role play some of their most frustrating pitches to see if you can help them see what went wrong. Don't forget to follow up your critiques with an encouraging word to show them that you're aware of their past successes and that you know they can repeat them in the future. Consider sharing a personal story of when you were in a similar situation and explain how you moved past whatever gave you problems.

CHAPTER 6

Conversation Starters: Small Talk for Big Opportunities

People buy people, not products or services. That's why word of mouth advertising is so incredibly valuable. People buy from people they know, like and trust. They don't develop that trust until they get to know you, and they don't get to know you until they've had a chance to talk to you and build a relationship. Building a relationship with a prospect or customer is a lot like making friends and building relationships anywhere. It starts with 'small talk.' You've got to:

1. **Make a good first impression.** Relax, smile, look people in the eye, be genuine.
2. **Let go of any judgments about the person you're meeting.** Don't focus on their clothes, their age, race, sexual orientation, body type or appearance. Don't dismiss or prejudge someone because of their looks. You really can't judge a book, or a person, by their cover.
3. **Pay attention.** Pay attention to the person, to anyone with them, to their environment, their clothing (not in

a judgmental way), and everything that is happening around them. Are they in a suit? Or surf shorts? Are they wearing a T-shirt with a photo or slogan on it that you can ask them about? Do they have military or other tattoos that might have a story behind them? If you have the chance to Google someone, or their company before speaking with them, do so. Learn as much as you can about them before you meet them when possible. Use that information as an icebreaker. If they've just come into your store or showroom, notice their demeanor. Do they seem rushed or relaxed? Are they 'just looking' or do they head directly to a certain section of the store? Simply saying, "You seem like you're in a hurry. May I help you?" lets them know you value their time and thus sparks trust.

4. **Be genuinely interested and curious about people.** Ask questions. Don't interrogate, but do pursue your curiosity. A great place to do this is in lines at stores. People generally welcome small talk to make the time pass. Ask about an item in their shopping cart. Ask them if they like it, or what they like about it. You can practice these skills anywhere.

You know now that good relationships are where the best sales opportunities lie. But breaking the ice with a potential customer can be one of the hardest things to do, for one or more reasons:

You're shy, introverted or not really a people person

Shy and introverted people actually make some of the best sales-people because they naturally shut up and let the customer talk and generally think about what they want to say before they say it. If you're not a people person you can learn to be with practice.

You haven't thought about sales as a conversation before. Old habits die hard. If you've been in sales for a long time you may find it difficult, confusing, or even scary to change the way you approach prospects.

You are afraid to be vulnerable. Most of us have been taught all our lives to protect ourselves, to not open up, to not be vulnerable. That's understandable in the corporate world or where being vulnerable can be risky. But the fact is, it's that vulnerability and willingness to open up to customers that helps us establish trust. When people see we're willing to be vulnerable with them they think, "He must trust me. It's safe to trust him back." It's our vulnerability, openness and willingness to share ourselves with others that creates the emotional connections we need for a successful sales relationship.

You don't like or 'do' chit-chat. Not everyone likes chit-chat. Many salespeople like to get right down to business, but not every customer does. The problem with not liking to talk to people can come across as judgmental, alienating or like you feel annoyed or bothered by the customer's questions or conversation.

You don't understand various social styles

You may be aware that introverted and extroverted people are different. Introverts tend to be quiet, avoid being the center of attention and listen more than talk. Extroverts tend to thrive on being with people, talking and being the center of attention. But there are other social styles to consider as well.

Because people are different and relate to others depending on their social style and personality, the same conversation starters don't work for all customers. There are four social styles, or personality types of customers — Analyticals, Drivers, Amiables, and Expressives. We all have characteristics of each style, but we tend to have one dominant style, especially when it comes to buying.

Each personality tends to buy based on their personality style. For instance, 'Analyticals' tend to like lots and lots of facts, details, case studies, and proven examples. They can never have too much information. They tend to be highly organized and are rarely swayed by an emotional argument. Their approach to buying is always thoughtful, logical and analytical. They're traditional fence sitters, guilty of paralysis by analysis. It's not that they don't or won't buy, but that they need a lot of details about the product before they buy. The good news is, once they make the decision to buy, they're totally in. They'll tend to buy any other peripheral or special offers, accessories or maintenance supplies as well. Contrast the Analytical with the 'Driver.'

Give a driver too much information and you'll turn them off. They view their time as valuable and precious and not to be wasted with lengthy presentations. They don't want to be your buddy. They want to know how competent you are and how you can solve their problem. They respond well to assertive presentations without a lot of details. If they want details, they'll ask for them. They make decisions quickly and first impressions mean everything. Give them clearly defined, concise options. Don't ramble.

Expressives love thrills, dreams, and the emotional sensations of buying. They don't want to miss out on being the first one to own a new product, or experience a new service. They respond well to having their dreams, visions and hopes supported and to feeling inspired by a product. They are emotionally involved in the sales process and want you to be as well. They like anecdotes, stories and examples as well personal stories you can share. They don't like a lot of detail, but love a lot of emotion.

Amiables want to be your friend before they buy. They are reluctant buyers who tend to have 'buyer's remorse' and are only less reluctant to buy than an Analytical personality. They're strong people persons, and like to see you are empathetic and interested in their challenges and problems and eager to help them solve them. They hate a hard sell or being pressured. They don't like conflict or feeling like they've been backed into a corner. Your presentation should be personal and specific to them and their concerns.

As you can see, breaking the ice starts before you even begin trying to strike up a conversation. Learn to identify the personality types you'll be dealing with, then figure out your noble purpose and discover your sales story.

Start with a Noble Sales Purpose

When Jason Goldberg, Founder and CEO of Ideal Life, started his business in 2002, he did so to make life better for family members. He had a vision for better health for his elderly relatives, some of whom were not only in declining health, but living thousands of miles away from his home in Toronto. Jason and his family worried about how to keep a watchful eye on their loved ones or to help them manage their various chronic conditions at a distance. What the Goldbergs discovered was they were not alone.

An estimated 133 million Americans are currently living with one or more chronic conditions. And for each of those 133 million Americans, there are 133 million or more caregivers who are worried about their loved ones.

Jason and his father, Harvey Goldberg, a consumer product and marketing expert (and former principle force behind the hugely successful Creepy Crawlers™ and Teddy Ruxpin™ toys of the '80s and '90s) already had the marketing and business experience. Now they had a noble cause. They just needed a product. So Jason began a systematic exploration of the healthcare marketplace, devoting two years to extensive field research. He did more than just read the literature and research. He conducted interviews with consumers, as well as medical professionals, engineers, and healthcare executives. He attended conferences and technology shows. He not only honed his ideas for new products and services that could fulfill the promise of remote health management, he focused on the end user and how to solve their specific health challenges. His noble cause was monitoring the health and safety of loved ones. What he came up with were products and software applications that allow doctors and family members to monitor a patient's or family member's health status wirelessly, in the comfort of their own homes. His small devices can monitor and relay information about heart conditions, COPD, diabetes, chronic congestive heart problems, high blood pressure, and weight control. The best part about his products, say the nurses, doctors, and health educators who use them, is that they can not only tell when a patient is feeling ill, but that that is the best time to educate them because they're most receptive to education then.

Not only are his products now leading the field in the telehealth and telemedicine field, they're saving lives. Ideal Life doesn't have to do much convincing. They let the people whose lives they've saved tell it for them. They videotape interviews with people who have benefitted from their product. That's where the story lies. It's been a very effective strategy, but a labor of love as well.

"That's why we started this company," Jason says. "We looked for a solution, but it didn't exist. So we listened to what people were asking for, came up with a practical and affordable solution, and then built that system from the ground up."

"The mission behind IDEAL LIFE really seemed to strike a chord," Jason says. "The team was passionate about the potential of healthcare information technology, and excited to be a part of the health IT 'revolution.'"

The Goldbergs and their employees and consultants get it. As Jason said, "The team was passionate about the potential of healthcare information technology, and excited to be a part of the health IT 'revolution.'"

If your sales goal is all about numbers, you're not only missing the point, you're most likely missing the sale. Helping your customer solve their problem, whether it's weight loss, monitoring their health, getting organized, remodeling a room in their home, or streamlining their business, you have to have both a noble purpose and sales staff and employees who embrace it. Many people may see "noble selling" as an oxymoron, but it's not. Customers are people, not targets to be acquired, or wallets to plunder.

Figure out what problems your product or service solves or can solve. Noble Sales purposes are the things that drive a company's employees to love their job.

Like the Goldbergs, Lisa Earle McLeod understands the importance of Noble Purpose. In her book, *Selling with Noble Purpose: How to Drive Revenue and Do Work that Makes You Proud*, McLeod writes about what a major biotech firm learned six years ago — that their top sales people had a greater sense of purpose than their average sales counterparts. In other words, they were not only passionate about their product; they saw their work as having meaning and purpose. The study was a six-month double-blind study of its sales force in order to determine what behaviors separated the top salespeople from the average ones. No one expected to discover that the best salespeople were the ones who truly want to make a difference to customers. They wanted to 'help,' to change lives, to make a difference. They consistently outsold salespeople who focused solely on sales goals and money.

As the Goldbergs and others have discovered, "Selling with noble purpose" turns out to be not only more successful, but hugely more profitable. Employees report greater job satisfaction and longevity at their jobs and customer service improves because people truly do want to do a better job.

What the Goldbergs and other companies have learned is that its easy to build your own list of conversation starters specific to your business by starting with your company's noble purpose.

Examples of noble purposes:

- Help families monitor their loved one's diabetes, heart and blood pressure problems from a distance
- Help customers lose weight
- Help customers streamline their businesses
- Help customers get organized
- Help customers...... what else?

See a keyword here? It's help! Find a way to convert what you do into a "helping" phrase and chances are you've found your noble purpose.

Build Your Dreams (BYD) founder Wang Chuanfu didn't go from being the son of poor Chinese farmers to billionaire and the world's largest cell phone battery manufacturer simply because he saw a great business opportunity. Wang had a noble cause, and a great story. He also genuinely cared about his customers and understood what it meant to be poor, to struggle, and to work hard.

Wang was 13 when his parents died. He was raised by the oldest of his seven siblings after his father, a carpenter, and then his mother, passed away. He graduated from high school, went to Beijing and with the financial backing of his brothers and sisters, attended and graduated from the University in Beijing before founding his own company.

Wang's billion dollar idea was to convert the world to electric vehicles to save the environment and reduce dependency on oil. He began with two goals — One, to use technology to provide better things for society, the world and the future, while also encouraging society to change in a good way. Two, he wanted to make electric cars for the masses that anyone could afford to purchase (noble purpose). Since Chinese private citizens were only allowed to start owning cars in 1995, the year Wang started his business, his noble purpose most likely played a very important role in his sales and growth.

China is now the world's largest importer of oil, having passed U.S. oil consumption a few years ago. Even with only a six percent penetration rate in private transportation, they already have a major air pollution problem. That pollution rate will get worse if the number of cars on the roads increases dramatically. If every Chinese citizen suddenly all bought cars, the problems in China would get so much worse, but Wang wants to prevent this. In spite of being accused of not delivering on his promise of electric cars, Wang is not flustered. He points out in numerous interviews that he needs the battery technology and energy storing solutions now, before the solar industry explodes. "If we wait until that happens," he told reporters at Caixin.com in 2011, "We'll be too late."

He knew what he was talking about. Three years later BYD is the world's largest electric bus maker in the world. They also own every step of their manufacturing process right down to the mines where the materials for their batteries come from. Wang's goals have now changed slightly. He wants to be the largest automaker in China by 2015. If anyone has a great story to tell, it's Wang.

Have a Story

Stories are merely our personal experiences shaped into a recounting or retelling of the event along with any insights, emotions or thoughts we have, or had, about the experience. Think about the last time you couldn't wait to tell a friend about something that happened at work, or on a first date, or at school, or a vacation. What did you feel when you were telling your friend about what happened? Did you raise your voice? Get excited? Did you wave your hands around or use body language to demonstrate some aspect of the event? Did you have a beginning, middle and end? Did you look for a reaction from your friend when you finished telling them what happened? If you did any of these things you were telling a story.

Todd's pastor convinced Todd, a local deacon at his church, to volunteer at a local soup kitchen feeding the homeless one weekend a month. He encouraged Todd to bring his family along for the experience. Todd felt apprehension and more than a little fear at the idea. He didn't know or understand homeless people. He wanted to see what his family would all be in for before committing them to the experience. Fortunately Todd's first day went well. He was surprised at what a good time he had talking to the residents and hearing how they became homeless. Suddenly, Todd was excited and signed up to volunteer again. He went home that night and told his family about his experience. He eventually convinced other church members to donate their time to the shelter. That noble purpose became part of Todd's sales story.

Can you see now how to use your noble purpose to create your sales story? You don't have to volunteer at a homeless shelter or rescue puppies, but you do need to find something you're passionate about and that is preferably related to your job. You want a sales story rather than a sales pitch because it's stories that stir people to action. Pitches shut them down. Stories are emotional connections to real events, real feelings, real fears and joys. They're not reports, they're not spreadsheets or bullet point slide presentations. They're actual events that reveal our vulnerability, our weaknesses, and our less than perfect abilities. They're a recounting of events that make us real. As the famous lines from the children's book, *The Velveteen Rabbit*, go:

"Generally, by the time you are Real, most of your hair has been loved off, and your eyes drop out and you get loose in the joints and very shabby. But these things don't matter at all, because once you are Real you can't be ugly, except to people who don't understand."

Stories help people relate and connect to you. Above all people want to feel safe. They want to trust that they won't be taken advantage of, humiliated, shamed, or bullied by the people and companies they do business with. What Michael Bosworth and Ben Zoldan explain in their book:

What Great Salespeople Do: The Science of Selling through Emotional Connection and the Power of Story, is how great leaders throughout history have understood this human trait, and relied on the power of story and vulnerability to change history.

Lincoln used his storytelling ability to sell abolition. Defense attorneys use storytelling to convince juries their client is innocent, and prosecutors use story to convince jurors the defendant is guilty. Oftentimes verdicts come down to who tells the best story. When we're pulled over by the police, or make a mistake at work we automatically fall back on our storytelling ability to craft a reason or story to influence the police officer, our boss or our co-workers about why we speeding, or failed to finish our report on time. We do this because we know people respond to stories. They may not always respond in the way we hope, but we know if our story is good, it will influence the outcome in some favorable way.

Great thought leaders, including those give some of the best and most popular TED talks, know that commonality makes the emotional connection. Great stories draw the listener or reader in with details that affirm or support what the listener already believes or wants to believe. Being able to identify with the speaker is just one more thing that helps them bond with the storyteller. It's why politicians adopt the accents, mannerisms and sometimes even the dress of the area of the country and the audience they're speaking with.

New processes and products are hard to sell simply because people don't identify with them. If what you're selling is different, or runs counter to what your customer is used to, you've got to find the few points they can identify with and slowly introduce them to the ones they don't care for.

Great storytellers don't change opinions, they open minds. They bring honesty, trust and solutions to the table. They don't overwhelm their audience with facts, they connect with relationship.

Akio Morita isn't exactly a household name in most American homes, but almost everyone recognizes the name 'Sony.' After World War II, Akio Morita was one of the co-founders of Sony. During his start-up phase, Morita visited the United States. As he toured different plants and spoke to various departments, he was struck by the mobility of employees between American companies. The freedom to change jobs and move from one company to another was unheard of in Japan at that time. Morita crafted a story about the advantages American workers and companies enjoyed because of this mobility. When he returned to Japan, he encouraged experienced, middle-aged employees of other companies to reevaluate their careers and consider joining Sony. It's how he was able to build up his company quickly using experienced workers.

How to Create a Strong Story

Just days away from a frontal lobotomy that would have left him dull, without the ability to show or feel emotions, Sherwin Nuland, M.D., was saved by a story an intern used to convince doctors that electro-shock therapy could cure the doctor. Everything else had been tried, so to appease the gifted young intern, the doctors allowed him to proceed with a series of electro-shock treatments on Dr. Nuland. The treatment worked. Dr. Nuland went from being a 'hopeless' depressive locked up in a mental ward to being able to practice medicine again. What worked for him could work for others, if he could convince the medical establishment to forget the horror stories of electro-shock therapy and see the benefits. How did he do that? In his TED talk he used his personal story of his decline and eventual healing. http://www.ted.com/talks/sherwin_nuland_on_electroshock_therapy

When we tell stories, we active the right side, the creative and more receptive side of our customers' brains as well as our own. Stories also don't make customers feel like they're being threatened or "sold to."

How to Craft Your Story

Crafting a story isn't about learning a script. It's not about making something up either. When telling a story to a customer it needs to be real. You must be genuine when talking to your customer. You're not trying to trick, manipulate or use them. You're trying to connect with them. Crafting a story is about sharing a personal, meaningful and relevant story about something you've experienced that will help you connect with your customer.

Think about the people or friends you know who tell great stories at parties, conferences, or get-togethers. What makes what they're saying so compelling? Is it the sequence of events? The tone of voice? The body language? Try tape recording yourself telling a story. Play it back and listen to your tone, the speed at which you talk, and any 'ums' or 'ahs' or pauses in your story. What parts of your story are interesting? Boring? Relevant?

When you talk to a customer you want your story to relate to their challenge or problem. So, you may end up adapting your story to emphasize one point over another. When Steve, a shoe salesman, was telling a story about his last hiking trip to a customer who was looking at hiking boots. He mentioned how sturdy the shoes were, but said he hated the weight of them. The customer agreed with the weight issues of sturdy boots. He asked if Steve knew of any company that made lighter weight boots.

Steve showed him several lightweight brands. He then explained that unless someone had weak ankles, or the trail was very rocky or uneven, or the person was not carrying a lot of weight, that another footwear option was a sturdy pair of sneakers. One thing led to another and soon Steve and his customer were swapping notes about different local trails and which ones he recommended or thought were safe to hike in sneakers, and which ones should be hiked in boots. He ended up selling four pairs of shoes to his customer who saw the value of different footwear for different conditions after their talk.

Your stories don't have to be best-sellers or potential block busting movies. They just have to be real, relevant and directed at helping the customer solve their problem.

How to Tell a Story

All stories have a beginning, a middle, and an end. That is called 'the story structure.' If you want to make an impact, understand your audience — what they like, what they don't like, and what they want to know. Describe a future, or at least a happy ending. And finally, capture your audience's attention as soon as possible, either with an amazing fact, news story, or product benefit that will make them want to know more. They're more likely to ask questions, helping break the ice and open up the door for you to share a story about the product, or yourself.

1. **Build a structure.** The beginning sets what is, and establishes credibility. The middle contrasts what is and what could be; and the end tells how amazing the future will be with your idea, solution or insight.

2. **Understand what will resonate with your audience or customer.** Nancy Duart, author, speaker and storyteller, mentions Steve Jobs' well-known iPhone launch speech and Dr. Martin Luther King Jr.'s *"I Have a Dream Speech"* because of the power of each of those speeches to connect with her audience.

3. **"Imagine and poetically describe an amazing future."** The whole point of telling a story is to get to the happy ending. That happy ending can be a solution, a lesson, an insight or a positive change of circumstances. Whatever the ending is, make it believable, achievable and memorable.

4. **Capture your customer's attention ASAP.** Perhaps the most famous beginning in movie history is the introduction to the movie 'Star Wars':

"A long time ago in a galaxy far, far away...." the three paragraph introduction then pulls the audience in with a short, simple backstory:

> *"It is a period of civil war. Rebel spaceships, striking from a hidden base, have won their first victory against the evil Galactic Empire.*
>
> *During the battle, Rebel spies managed to steal secret plans to the Empire's ultimate weapon, the Death Star, an armored space station with enough power to destroy an entire planet.*
>
> *Pursued by the Empire's sinister agents,*

Princess Leia races home aboard her starship, custodian of the stolen plans that can save her people and restore freedom to the galaxy..."

Those three paragraphs prove you don't have to say much to launch your listener into a state of rapt attention right off the bat. The secret is in knowing what's important to the listener, and keeping your facts, setting and introduction short, relevant, simple and informative.

When you tell your story, often your story will spark a customer's story. Your goal is not to entertain and amuse your customer, but to engage him and prompt him to share his own stories. Remember, it's not a competition, it's a relationship. Swapping stories not only keeps the conversation going, it helps you get to know each other even more. Look for ways to contribute to the conversation to keep it moving. The more your customer talks, and the more stories he tells, the more you learn. The bonus is that if you're a good listener, the more the customer is likely to trust you with each new story one of you tells. If your customer isn't talking, chances are they aren't buying either.

Break the Ice and Establish Rapport

Now that you have your story, you're ready to break the ice. If you can do it successfully, humor is a good way to start. If humor isn't your thing, try honest compliments, or ask questions about a non-sales or non-product topic. Anything from the weather to a ring the customer is wearing, to a recent item in the news, sports, or upcoming holiday can be an icebreaker. The goal is to connect with the person and get them talking to you. Once you're talking and the ball is rolling you can shift or start a conversation about what problem or challenge they're trying to solve.

Don't just go through the motions to get to the part about where you talk about the product. See the person, not the profits. Focus on the customer as someone you can help first, and then sell. Ask questions to get to know them, not just to appear interested. Remember, they are people first, not just walking wallets.

- Ask what something means instead of just what it is
- What can you tell me about yourself / your business?
- What do you need / want?
- Find out about their interests
- Find out how they decided to come to you instead of a competitor
- Find out what their expectations are — do they believe there is a solution?
- Find out what they think their problem or challenge is — it may be different than what you think it is
- Don't assume anything. Just because other customers may like a particular feature or product benefit doesn't mean they will

Determine if the Customer Will Buy

Qualifying, or determining if the customer is a likely prospect and will buy from you, is about more than just figuring out if:

- They can afford your product or service
- If the person you're speaking with is the decision maker

- How likely they are to choose you over a competitor

It's also about determining if:

- **They really need your product.** Not everyone who walks in your door or buys your product needs it. I didn't realize this until I heard a salesman in a hardware store explaining to a customer that the spackle she was asking about was for filling large holes in plaster walls. What she needed, he said, was a different kind of spackle for filling nail holes. The product he recommended came in a smaller container, was less expensive and made exactly for what she needed it for. He may not have made the bigger sale that day, but I'm guessing she continued to come back and buy other products from him because he helped her solve her problem by getting her what she needed, not what he had to sell.
- **Are they a good fit for your product and company?** A customer who buys a product they don't really need and that doesn't truly help them solve their problem can cost you future business. The customer will assume you don't understand them or their problems and will take their business elsewhere. You may make one sale to that customer, but you won't make another.

After you've broken the ice and initiated a conversation with your prospect, some of the questions to ask in order to qualify them, or determine if they're ready and able to buy are:

- What do you wish you were able to do?
- What are your priorities?
- Are you looking at other options?

- How long have you been looking for a solution?
- What have you tried that hasn't worked?
- Have you tried anything that seemed to work, or partially worked?
- Is anything keeping you from acting today if I can find a solution for you?

Challenge and Guide the Buyer

What does it mean to challenge and guide the buyer? In *The Challenger Sale: Taking Control of the Customer Conversation*, authors Matthew Dixon and Brent Adamson discovered the key characteristics of a star sales rep, someone they call a "Challenger."

They graded more than 6,000 sales reps on 44 attributes. They found out that the highest performing profile, by a landslide, was one they called the "challenger."

According to Dixon and Adamson, challengers have the ability to:

- **Teach** the customer a new way to look at his or her own market and business issues.
- **Tailor** the solution to the specific issues that the customer faces.
- **Take control** of the conversation, thus leading the customer through the application of the insight to the customer's problem and the steps to transition from the current approach.

Customers actually seek out the challenger salesperson because they trust and value their advice, expertise and creativity and assertiveness. The challenger is not there just to make a sale, but to create a relationship that benefits the customer. Case in point:

Catalog sales are one of the most challenging sales fields of all. Not only are most of the sales made over the telephone, where you can't read your prospect's body language or make suggestions based on a visual interaction with the person, most people calling a catalog store have already made their list and made up their mind what they want. With the ones who haven't made up their minds, you have one chance to earn their trust and find a solution before they hang up. At many call centers you also have a limited amount of time to allot to each phone call. But it can be done.

An inbound sales call rep for a high-end women's fashion store received a call from one of her regular customers. The woman was a senior officer for a large corporation and traveled a lot on business. Her clothes were important. Over time, this customer had come to trust the rep's judgment and honesty and called with an urgent problem. She would be traveling to Egypt to spend time on an archeology dig with her college aged daughter who was there for the summer. She'd also play tourist before going onto Paris for business. Her usual routine when traveling was to mix and match her current wardrobe with what she'd need for the country she was visiting. When she left that country she simply donated the items she didn't need so she'd have room in her bags for any souvenirs she picked up along the way.

The rep knew this from the many conversations they'd had each time the woman ordered. The customer raved about the casualness of the dig and of being a tourist, but also shared that she wasn't sure how to pack for her Paris trip since it would entail a much higher end wardrobe. Money wasn't the issue; convenience was. The rep suggested the woman buy an entirely new wardrobe for Egypt, donate it to one or more of the students at the dig when she left Egypt and then buy a new wardrobe when she arrived in Paris with empty bags, but wearing the one business suit she'd wear on the plane. The noble cause was obvious — convenience, plus students at the dig would benefit from the clothes she left. Not only would she not have to worry about losing her wardrobe if the airlines lost her empty luggage, she would arrive in Paris with empty suitcases and a plan to fill with new clothes. The customer was thrilled with the solution and placed a several thousand dollar order.

Putting Conversation Starters into Action

In his book *Outliers*, Malcolm Gladwell talks about the factors that determine a person's, or a company's success. One of the things he discovered and repeatedly mentions throughout the book is the "10,000-Hour Rule." Gladwell claims that the key to success in any field is, to a large extent, a matter of practicing a specific task for a total of around 10,000 hours. Whether it's hockey, tennis, cooking, writing or playing a musical instrument, 10,000 hours seems to be the point at which most people become really good at what they do, no matter what it is. Starting a conversation is no different. It takes practice. The more you start up conversations with anyone, the better your ice breaking skills are going to be.

1. **Determine what your noble purpose is.** A noble purpose doesn't have to be something that will win you humanitarian of the year or a Pulitzer. It just has to be something that motivates you to make a difference, or that you believe makes a difference. It's not just about selling a product or service. A noble purpose is about making the world or a person's life better in some way.

2. **Think about some stories you could tell customers which they'd remember and which could spark interaction with them and, perhaps, a sale down the road.** If you don't already own and use whatever it is you're selling, perhaps now is the time to do that. If you're selling industrial equipment, spend time on the floor, talking to the people who use the equipment. Become familiar with the equipment and the people who use it. Ask them what they like, don't like about it. Get them to share their stories about the product.

3. **Break the ice through humor and/or asking potential new customers questions about themselves.** This can be something as simple as sharing photos of your pet, or asking them if they've seen the latest movie, or if they're a sports fan. This is another good reason to keep personal items and photos on your desk, to wear unique tie clips or jewelry or to notice the same items in your potential customer's office. More than a few sales have been made over the fact someone turned out to be an alum of the same school, shared a passion for scuba diving, skiing, tennis or french food.

4. **Ask them about their needs / wants.** One of the biggest mistakes salespeople make is listening with the intent to pair a specific need with the product instead of looking at the big picture and the overall solution. If a customer

comes into the store wanting to buy a $500 attachment for his riding lawnmower when a $150 weed-eater will do a better job, which one do you sell him? Price isn't always a customer's concern. Ask him if he has a budget. If it's not, or he's not certain, find out who will be using the mower or performing the task most. Is safety, weight, technical or skill ability an issue or concern? Help him explore the pros and cons of each, including price.

5. **As you get to know them, look for a place to tell your story after you learn a bit about them.** When telling a story, don't 'one-up' your customer. If they caught a 5-pound bass, don't tell them about your 10-pounder. Swapping stories isn't about competing to see who has the best or most extreme story. It's about sharing common experiences, such as the elation of catching the biggest fish of your life, winning a big game, or landing a dream job or having kids you love.

6. **Listen for their story and then look for a way to contribute.** Listening for story means more than just listening to the words. It means listening for the intent behind the story. Ask yourself why they're telling the story or stories they are. Are they talking a lot about their wife and kids? Maybe they're really proud of their family. You might want to say, "It sounds like you're really proud of your family." If they say they are, ask what they like best about having a family. Chances are that answer will have a lot to do with their motivation for considering your product.

7. **Guide the conversation by teaching your customer something, tailoring a solution, and then challenging them.** Studies show that customers gravitate towards salespeople who know their product's good points and bad, and who also know how to explain how to use the

product and when to use it. Lowes doesn't just hire anyone to sell their lumber, plumbing and electrical products. They hire people with unequalled product knowledge in their area, be it plumbing, tile or flooring. They don't just sell plumbing in the plumbing area. They sell solutions. They offer their expertise and experience.

The really good sales associates will even show you more effective or efficient solutions. Do the same. Go to Walmart or Kmart and you can buy any one of a dozen pots and pans at a great price, but good luck finding anyone who can explain the difference between ceramic and Teflon frying pans. If you're serious about cooking, you go to a store that specializes in cookware and that hires salespeople who love to cook and are knowledgeable about cooking. Make no mistake, people love to buy. They hate to be sold. When you answer your prospect's questions and help them understand your product because you want to help, not because you want to sell; chances are they'll buy.

Resources:
http://www.forbes.com/sites/hbsworkingknowledge/2014/01/02/what-warren-buffett-saw-in-newspapers/

CHAPTER 7
Awaken and Expand Your Network

	How many people are you currently connected with you through your online social networks (LinkedIn, Facebook, Google+, etc.)?
	How many of these people do or did you actually know in real life?
	How many of them do you make a constant effort to stay in touch with face-to-face?
	For the people in your networks who you don't know in real life, how many of them have you attempted to contact beyond accepting their connection request?
	Do you belong to any online thought leaderships groups? If so, do you participate in them?
	What kinds of people are included in your face-to-face network?

Sometime around the turn of the 20th century two of the country's most eccentric and brilliant men came together in an unexpected way. Mark Twain was at a club he frequented when Nikola Tesla came in. Both were already aware of each other's work, so they became natural friends. Tesla read Twain's work while he was laid up as a child, and Twain had followed Tesla's patent applications for some time. In fact, letters show that Twain had tried to buy some of Tesla's Austrian and English patents for a "destructive terror" he was working on. When they met for the first time, they had plenty to talk about, as Twain was in love with everything that had to do with science.

Twain was seen frequently at Nikola Tesla's lab, and the two often tested out experiments together, with Twain volunteering to be Tesla's guinea pig. In one particular case, a well-known, dramatic photo shows Twain holding one of Tesla's inventions, which was zapping him with electricity. Imagine the conversation that may have ensued:

"The machine's got therapeutic effects," Tesla said to Twain.

"Count me in," Twain said as he took hold of the machine. Tesla flipped it on.

"It's giving me 'vigor and vitality,'" Twain was quoted as having said.

After much shaking from holding onto the device, Twain suddenly drops it and runs for the restroom. Some have said jokingly that Tesla invented the electric laxative.

This fun story—and many others about the two men, in fact— was only possible through real in-person networking. The two men met at parties and / or at a club they both frequented and already had a mutual respect for others in their field. Because of their other connections, they were able to become friends.

We hear about a side of Twain other than the literary side we all know so well. Back then, there were no computers, no email, no Twitter, or Facebook, and phones were still in their infancy. Networking took time and energy, but when done right, amazing things happened.

Today, the concept of networking has taken on a whole new meaning. It's so easy to sit behind our computers and make so-called connections with people we have never met. But these certainly aren't real connections. They are nothing but lazy, feeble attempts to build a network which does nothing to help our goals. Can you really be connected to someone you've never met and have no intention of meeting face to face? Absolutely not. Real networking requires effort and work, just as it did in the days of Mark Twain and Nikola Tesla. It requires taking steps to build relationships with the people you want to get to know. As Australian billionaire businessman Lindsay Fox once said, "Personal relationships are always the key to good business. You can buy networking;" he said. "You can't buy friendships."

So how can you go about building real, personal relationships? It helps to first understand what has changed in networking habits.

How Networks are Different Today

Building out your network provides some immense opportunities. Networking is all about engagement with the people you meet. So what does engagement look like? If you're taking 100 percent of the responsibility for the relationship, then you should be a great listener. Guy Kawasaki, who has worked with numerous large technology companies like Apple and Google, once said,

"The mark of a good conversationalist is not that you can talk a lot. The mark is that you can get others to talk a lot. Thus, good schmoozers are good listeners, not good talkers."

We've already discussed some tips for improving your listening abilities. This should be something you're constantly working on no matter how good you think you already are. There's always room for improvement. The key is to pay attention and focus on the other person, excluding everything else, as you take in their story.

Engagement happens when the other person pauses and then becomes truly entranced with the idea of getting to know you. After all, how often do you run across someone who truly is a good listener? When was the last time you met someone who asked questions about you and listened to what you had to say?

We all love to be heard. It's too easy to allow others to draw us into talking about ourselves. However, you will find that you become a much better networker if you listen. After all, you already know everything about yourself. So take some time to find out everything you can about the people you meet. You'll probably not only learn about them but also discover interesting bits of trivia or other information that you didn't know before.

Building and using your network gives you a leg up in the sales process. How many times have you had a customer say to you, "My friend, Sam, referred me to you because she said you were the best"? If you've never heard anything like this before, there's a good chance that you're missing out on a lot of sales opportunities because you aren't building and expanding your network. The more people you know, the more people you have the potential to meet. And the more groups you interact with, the more opportunities you will have to meet people with whom you share common goals.

So how do you go about building a network that keeps working? In her book, *The Nanosecond Networlders*, Melissa G. Wilson, lists what she sees as the seven steps to building a solid and expansive network, which she calls your "Networld." She lists the seven steps as: establishing a values-rich foundation; making connections for your primary circle; expanding your circles; initiating exchanging relationships; growing and nurturing relationships; co-creating opportunities; and recreating your networld.

Wilson advises people to find some value, topic, or interest they have in common with new contacts and build on that. Then build your primary circle, which she says is made up of no more than 10 people you spend most of your time with. Next, you can expand your network by connecting with people who are connected to those in your primary circle. Fourth, you begin building relationships with whom you can exchange things with. Fifth, you take the time to grow and nurture your relationship by co-creating and exchanging opportunities with them, which is the sixth step. Finally, you should recognize that your networld will change and grow, which will require you to continue recreating it over time.

Face-to-Face Networking

I touched briefly on how face-to-face networking today has virtually disappeared because of technology. Connecting with people face to face is becoming a lost art, but it doesn't have to be. With some effort on your part, you can create long-lasting relationships that matter to those with whom you connect.

Multiple studies have shown just how important face-to-face networking is. I won't cover all of them, but one that's particularly interesting was conducted by The Maritz Institute, which published a white paper on the subject in September 2010. The white paper is titled *"The future of Meetings: The Case for Face-to-Face"* and is written by Mary Beth McEuen and Christine Duffy. Cornell University's Center for Hospitality Research also published the same paper as a perspective for the hospitality industry.

The paper focuses on how face-to-face meetings are essential in business relationships, particularly in the advent of face-to-face technology like Skype. Researchers discovered that there are three reasons situations in which face-to-face meetings are the best approach: "to capture attention;" "to inspire a positive emotional climate;" and "to build human networks and relationships."

The authors note a number of studies that focused on the return on investment of travel and meeting expenses in big businesses. Oxford Economics USA and Tourism Economics conducted one of the studies, entitled *The Return on Investment of U.S. Business Travel*, in 2009. In that case, they found that investment in business travel generated returns of between $10 and $14.99 for every dollar of investment. In other words, the relationships that were developed and cemented because of business travel ended up being more valuable, dollar-wise, than not taking a trip at all.

Forbes Insights conducted a separate study, also in 2009. Researchers in that case found that over 80 percent of executives actually prefer face-to-face meetings rather than virtual ones. The reasons why they preferred face-to-face contact varied. Of those who took part in the study, 85 percent of them said it helped them forge business relationships which were more meaningful. Seventy-seven percent of them said they were better able to read body language when face-to-face, and 75 percent of them said they were better able to socially interact and bond with both clients and co-workers when meeting face to face rather than virtually.

Both of these studies show that face-to-face meetings are important because they allow us to be more impactful. Researchers at the Maritz Institute used both of them as the basis for their study, then describing when face-to-face is better than virtual meetings. They said beginning a new relationship or changing the nature of a relationship is best done face to face because it allows you to capture the attention of the other person.

Of course this finding could be said about face-to-face meetings in general. It is easier to limit distractions in face-to-face meetings than it is in virtual ones because you're physically there with the other person. Often when we're sitting in front of a computer, we feel the need to multi-task, thus dividing our attention between the person we are meeting with and whatever else is going on. Researchers also discovered that meeting face-to-face helps break through the auto-pilot we often switch on because we stimulate more of the senses at the same time while focusing them all on one thing—the person we're meeting with.

Researchers at the Maritz Institute note that because of the increased attention, you're also able to inspire the other person, increasing their enthusiasm because of your excitement. This goes back again to being able to read the other person's body language better. The person you're meeting with can do the same to you, thus, making your body language more effective as well.

And third, meeting face-to-face simply makes it easier to build networks and relationships. People naturally want to feel connected, and when you're giving back to the other person regularly, this feeling of connectedness increases exponentially by meeting face to face. After all, as writer Deepak Chopra said, "Giving connects two people, the giver and the receiver, and this connection gives birth to a new sense of belonging." The more the other person feels like they belong in a business relationship with you, the better that relationship will be.

So how can we make the most of face-to-face meetings? It essentially boils down to making sure that you're listening effectively to the client and that distractions for the client are minimized as much as you can do so. This will enable the client to listen to you more closely as well.

It ranges from impossible (in the case of text posts) to nearly impossible (in Skype meetings, etc.) to read the other person's body language. As a result, a key part of making the most of all your face-to-face meetings is keeping a close watch on the client's body language. There is so much to miss out on if you don't have the opportunity to see a client move and respond to your conversation in person. In the case of text messages and email, you can't hear the other person's tone of voice, which can lead to some big misunderstandings. If you connect through a social network like LinkedIn without making an effort to get to know the other person, then that connection is completely wasted.

Here are some other tips for making the most of your face-to-face time:

- **Make a good first impression** – Whenever you show up to a meeting with someone, whether it's the first or the 50th, you should show interest in what they're saying. Smile and make eye content and have a confident handshake.

- **Don't be a pushy salesperson** – Your first thought when it comes to networking events, conferences, and parties should not be making a hard sell. Instead you should be thinking about how to get to know the other person better. If you try hard to make a sell while at one of these events, then you look desperate and people will be far less inclined to get to know you. They will think that being in a relationship with you will mean that you are constantly trying to get them to buy something.

- **Follow up** – The biggest reason business relationships fall apart is lack of follow-up. When following up with people, it should be timely and relevant. You'll rarely see any business from people you meet only once. Every contact doesn't have to be face to face, especially in the beginning, but if you don't do a face-to-face follow-up, then you should at least drop the other person an email or pick up the phone. Just make sure that you keep in contact with the other person because successful business relationships are not built in a day.

- **Be memorable** – This can sometimes be the biggest challenge for salespeople. Whenever you're hired or trained for a specific job, you're essentially given a script and some guidelines and told to adhere to them. However, you can still personalize what your business gives you. One of the best ways to be memorable is simply to know who you are and why you are unique. Then find ways to help others remember who you are. At big events, some people even wear their nametags upside down so that people will really pay attention to their names. I keep a special nametag for such events. The nametag can be personalized to make it more memorable than the plain white sticky nametags typically handed out at conventions. One person I met always wears hats to big events so that he easily stands out in a crowd. Others have some sort of introductory line that's unforgettable. Do whatever allows you to express your personality while also making yourself memorable to the people you meet.

Online Networking

Because of how popular online networking has become, I'll focus a significant chunk of what's left of this chapter on this segment of online networking. Because of the Internet, we can connect with potential clients all over the world. This creates immeasurable opportunities to share and connect. Those who don't use their online networks are missing out in so many ways.

So how can you make the most of your online network? It all starts with what you share. Actor Edward Norton said, "Instead of telling the world what you're eating for breakfast, you can use social networking to do something that's meaningful." Of course, what's meaningful to one person may not mean anything to the next, so it's helpful to learn different techniques for meeting, sharing with, and interacting with people in your online net-works. As a guideline, we'll look at some ideas for connecting with both people you know and don't know.

For Someone You Know

In some cases, you may have connected with someone you have met a time or two through LinkedIn or one of the other social networks. In other cases, you may have allowed a relationship to slump by ignoring it or being complacent about it. Whatever the reason you feel like you want to develop a relationship with someone you know, there are some simple ways to go about it.

The whole process is really very simple. Just show interest in the other person. As Dale Carnegie once said, "You can make more friends in two months by becoming interested in other people than you can in two years by trying to get other people interested in you."

So show that you're interested in the person you want to get to know, using your online link to do so. When you reach out though, make sure that you're genuine. Be genuinely interested in what the other person has to say. Also show gratitude when they respond to you. If you've reached out correctly, chances are good that they will indeed respond. And don't forget to offer to help. Remember, you're taking 100 percent responsibility for the relationship, so you should offer to help without expecting anything in return.

It's good to have a general script in mind when you do this. Here are the basic elements of a proper script:

1. A personalized welcome.
2. A suggestion to connect for a mutually beneficial relationship.
3. And a thank you for reading your message / accepting your connection request, or whatever else makes sense here.

This script is so basic that you can use it in any situation with someone you know, even at multiple phases of the relationship. The main reason it is so basic is because you already know some things about the other person, so you have something upon which to build and develop your relationship. As you craft your script, think about the things you have in common with the other person and relate them somehow to your suggestion to connect. Remember to keep the message very personal rather than just making a generic script for this. If you're not adapting it to each and every message you send, then you're doing it wrong.

For Someone You DON'T KNOW

If you're trying to get to know someone you've never met before, then the script will obviously go quite a bit differently. You'll need more of an introduction because neither you nor the other person knows anything about each other. You don't have some commonality upon which to build because this is someone you haven't met before. However, if you're the one making the first move, then you've probably read the other person's online profile. If so, then there's a reason you felt compelled to reach out to the other person. You may have noticed some sort of commonality upon which to build, but you've then got to introduce that commonality to the other person before you can move forward. Here are the basic building blocks of a script to introduce yourself to someone you have never met:

1. A personalized introduction.
2. In the body of the message, identify something in the person's profile that you either find interesting or have in common.
3. Suggest connecting for a mutually beneficial relationship.
4. Thank them for taking the time to read your invitation.
5. Suggest a "next step" to connect further.

A connection message written to someone you don't know should be even more detailed than one written to someone you do know. You should demonstrate that you have put some thought into contacting them directly and that you truly think that there is some way you can both help each other. The key words here are "mutually beneficial relationship."

Once again though, don't forget to take 100 percent responsibility for the relationship. Offer something to them rather than asking something from them. You are much more likely to get a response if you offer something, but do it in such a way that you don't come off sounding like there's some sort of gimmick. You want to target people you can make exchanges with so that the relationship does not become one-sided.

However, don't expect to receive anything in return from the other person, at least not right away. Harvey Mackay, a well-known motivational speaker, has said, "My golden rule of networking is simple: don't keep score." Take the initiative and be a giver in the beginning, without keeping track of how much you think the other person owes you. Over time, if the other person isn't just a taker, they will naturally start giving back to you. The more you develop and expand your network, the more mutual opportunities for both the other person and yourself you will discover.

Grow Your Influence through Online Groups

So where might you meet people who would be good additions to your network? Perhaps the simplest way is to approach them through LinkedIn by using a mutual connection. However, the mutual connection must be someone you already have a good face-to-face relationship with. If you don't have a relationship with your mutual connection and don't feel like that connection is a good person to add into your real network (not your virtual one), then it may be best to not even acknowledge that you both know the same person. The topic could come up in conversation at some point if you ask how the person you're connecting with how they know the person you both know. But if it does, it should be later in the relationship, possibly as a talking point a few conversations in.

Aside from simply running across their profile on LinkedIn, you could also join some groups. No matter where you are in your career, you can benefit greatly from joining groups, both in the real world and on LinkedIn. Even people who are very successful in their careers fine a benefit in joining groups. Best-selling author Nora Roberts said benefits tremendously. "I believe strongly in writing groups such as Romance Writers of America that offer support, information, and networking," she has said in the past.

The benefit of joining groups where you actually show up for meetings is that you're already in face-to-face situations with the people you meet and share with. The challenge is making yourself memorable because at big events, you meet so many people that it's impossible to remember everyone you meet.

On the other hand, one benefit of joining groups on social networks like LinkedIn is that you have the opportunity to meet significantly more people than you do at big conferences. A second is that you can spread your influence further because you can make comments in a place where more people will have the chance to see them and respond to you, thus making more connections possible. The challenge of joining and participating in groups on LinkedIn is taking the relationships you form on the social network to the next level so that you're meeting regularly with the other person face to face.

When it comes to online groups, there is nearly an endless supply. So how do you go about choosing which groups to become a member of? Here are some things to look for. You might consider industry-specific groups like healthcare, retail, or something else. The group should be a place where you can meet potential customers or where you have something in common with the people who belong to the group.

There are also local and regional groups, which can be of great benefit because you have more opportunities for getting to know the members on a face-to-face basis. And then there are solution-specific groups.

In addition to looking for a specific kind of group, you should also look for one in which you can position yourself as a resource or industry professional. Look for conversations in the groups that you can contribute to with informed answers and solutions for the problems that are presented. Look for questions to which you can provide a full answer.

Also look for opportunities to share high quality content. Some of this content may be your own, things you have written or presentations you have given. But I caution you about only sharing your own work, as this can make you seem narcissistic and like you are advertising yourself rather than helping people. Instead, mix your own work with links and webinars given by other people. Post links to content that helped you with a similar question to what was posted.

Making Connections through Groups

After you've determined what kinds of groups to join, it's time to start engaging with those groups and the individuals who belong to them. Don't wait for someone to engage with you because that nearly never happens. You must be the one to engage first. After all, as entrepreneur Christine Comaford-Lynch said, "Networking is marketing. Marketing yourself, marketing your uniqueness, marketing what you stand for."

So now think for a moment about how you are marketing yourself within the groups you're joining. You've got to have a certain type of packaging to appeal to your ideal customers, just like the products that you sell. Often customers see the person selling the products more than they see the products themselves, especially if they require a great deal of explanation. Networking enables you to explain your products better, but as you meet people, make sure that the way you market yourself is positive.

Clients look for salespeople who have integrity and are honest. They usually know if people are being honest or just making sales talk. Clients don't like sales pitches because they often feel the product that's being offered isn't reliable. And since they don't like sales pitches, you can pretty much bet that they won't like you if you're making a sales pitch when introducing yourself. Just try to sound natural and friendly when introducing yourself to someone new. As you build each relationship, your goal is to implant thoughts that you can be trusted into the minds of those you meet. Remember, trust is earned over a long period of time. It doesn't happen overnight.

As you scope out the groups you have joined for people to add to your network, you should constantly be looking for ways to help others. If you think someone could become a client down the road, think about where the person will need the product you are selling. If you can't figure it out and you have nothing in common with that person, then maybe they aren't your best option as an addition to your network.

So get out there and market yourself within the group. Remember though, while a sale is your end goal, this should be tucked in the back of your mind while you're getting to know people. Ask questions of the group to see who responds and answer questions to which you have a complete solution. LinkedIn has some excellent groups and a great platform to establish yourself as an expert and thought leader in your area of expertise. People who belong to the groups ask questions and engage with each other through the group. As you get to know the group itself and some of the people in it, look at the members' profiles and request a connection, indicating that you are a member of the same group they are.

Be a People Person

Right now I know some people are telling themselves that they aren't a "people person" and have no talent in networking. But if you're going to be a successful salesperson, then you must become a people person. You should be able to get along with people no matter their race, age, education level, gender, peculiarities or anything else. If you pale at the thought of networking, it is still possible to learn how to be comfortable meeting others. And believe it or not, if you're able to get along with all kinds of people, everything else will fall naturally into place. But you won't find all the answers to becoming a better conversationalist in this book. Instead, you've got to get out there and observe people who are excellent at talking to anyone and everyone. Another great thing about networking, particularly in groups you join, is that you can meet people who are able to talk to anyone about anything and learn from them. Perhaps in one particular case, the "sale" you're looking for is actually the other person helping you learn how to talk to anyone you want to talk to. If you can find the right person to (probably unknowingly) teach you this, then you'll have an opportunity to exchange some of your skills with them.

The more comfortable you become in your group, the more advanced your skills will become. You'll start to notice that some people in the group don't like to listen, while others prefer to listen. It's best to strike a balance in between and learn how to appeal to both types of people.

And as you meet people in the group and talk to them, remember; make sure you don't sound like you're trying to land a sale, even though that's your end purpose. If you sound too much like a salesperson when you meet the first few people in the group, soon you'll notice them start to nudge each other when you approach and then move away (either in the real world or virtually). It's impossible to build your network if you've driven people away because all you talk about is trying to get them to buy something.

Subtlety will be your friend in these cases. This is something that takes practice because it can be difficult to strike the perfect balance of aiming for a sale without letting on in the beginning that it's what you're doing. For example, if you're a real estate agent, you could work a conversation toward a particular property you're selling that you think the other person could be interested in. You could tell them about a place you've visited. If you've listed the property, then you've been there, so it isn't a lie. Talk about how beautiful it is, and then if someone asks where it is, you can talk about it without sounding like you were trying to get into a sales talk.

Putting this into Action

1. **Don't shirk face-to-face time.** The best way to keep in contact with the people you meet is to give them a call from time to time and ask to meet face to face. An email also works, although phone calls are better because it helps the other person remember who you are by hearing

your voice. If you don't meet with the people in your network face to face on a regular basis, you will find that your relationships begin to wilt.

2. **Always be genuine when interacting with others.** People sense when you're being fake, so don't even try to be real if you don't feel it. No one wants to add those they feel are just putting up a fake front to their network because these types of people do not make good connections. Be genuinely interested in others and use subtlety to guide natural conversations to the place you want them to be.

3. **Find ways to make yourself memorable to those you meet.** This is especially true at big networking events where you meet hundreds of new people. Wear a hat that describes your personality, keep a special nametag for these events, or do something else that makes you stand out from the crowd.

4. **Show gratitude.** Always thank the people you reach out to as potential additions to your network. Thank them for reading your message, for accepting your connection request, and anything else that is appropriate.

5. **Suggest connecting for a mutually beneficial relationship.** Most people have online networks that they never use and don't have any intention to use. In order to break that habit, you'll have to be the first one to reach out and suggest that you connect for a mutually beneficial relationship. If you have met the person you're trying to connect with before, then use what you already know to build a foundation in your connection request before suggesting that you can help each other.

6. **When trying to connect with someone you don't know, introduce yourself.** It takes a bit more of an introduction to connect with others you don't know, but it can

be done. If the person is a second-degree connection, use your mutual connection to start the person talking, but only if you know the middle person well enough to be able to talk about the person. If the person you're trying to connect with is not a second-degree connection, tell them what you see in their profile that interests you and then introduce yourself, explaining what you have in common and suggesting that you can help each other.

7. **Target a few different types of groups you would like to join.** Groups are an excellent way to expand your network. Take some time considering what types of groups would benefit you, and then start looking for those groups. Social networks provide an excellent place to find these groups.

8. **Use online groups to grow your influence.** After you join some online groups, engage with the other group members by answering questions, asking questions, and just taking part in the conversations. Share helpful content within the group as well, mixing some of what you might have done with the work of others.

9. **Be the first to engage with the individuals you want to meet.** In most cases on online networks, people are pretty complacent in terms of their face-to-face relationships with the people in their networks. Be the first to reach out if you want to have a real, mutually beneficial relationship with someone in your network or someone who belongs to the same group as you.

CHAPTER 8

Action Steps to Take Conversations to the Next Level

By now you must be asking yourself: is this a book about sales or about relationships? The answer is both! You can't have a million dollar sales conversation without a relationship. In fact, once you become skilled at developing relationships, million dollar sales conversations just sort of happen—almost without any noticeable effort on your part.

But in reality, you do put effort in when you do things honestly. You pour your heart and soul into a relationship in a way that was so natural you didn't even feel in the beginning that you were aiming for a million dollar sales conversation. The most lucrative conversations are those that happen naturally as a result of a good relationship built on a solid foundation of trust and exchange.

The Domino Effect

If you only remember one thing from this book, remember that sales are all about relationships. Think of it like a massive, intricate domino set-up. Start with a great relationship, and the rest of the steps will fall naturally into place if you put time and effort into it. Each step in this book builds upon the next. As one domino touches the next, it touches the next one, and so on—all the way through the chain.

And a relationship is the first domino.

Step 1: A is for Attitude

In order to have good relationships, you must have a good attitude. People enjoy the company of positive people who want to help them—not just sell something to them. If you want to be successful, you must take 100 percent responsibility for the relationship. The best way to sell yourself is by helping first. Put other people first, and they will sense that there's something different about you.

Avoid having a defensive attitude, or you'll be putting customers on the defensive. Respond to what they say rather than react by thinking through your response before you give it. Look for ways to expand your opportunities and ask questions without assuming anything. Look for opportunities to collaborate with your customers, building a partnership relationship.

Don't forget that all relationships are unique, so take the time to personalize them. Keep in touch with your contacts on a regular basis, even sending them a note or calling them just to check in. Set regular meeting dates with your contacts to keep the relationship rolling. And if a potential new customer shows up asking for advice about what your competitor recommended, don't be afraid to look and share. Even if you don't win that sale, you'll have established a relationship that will most likely bring the customer right back to you.

Step 2: Set Goals and Stick to Them

If you have a good attitude, it will be easy for you to write down your goals and achieve them. Studies show that people who are more positive, who believe they can achieve their goals and remain focused on them, are much more likely to achieve their goals. Each day, examine your goals to remind yourself of them and see how they intersect with the goals your contacts have set. Take 100 percent responsibility for all your relationships first, and then take 100 percent responsibility for your own success. Notice that others come first, but write down your goals so that you never lose sight of them—no matter what's going on in your life.

When you have goals set in stone and look at them every day, you remain motivated to stick with them. You're also able to look at your relationships through the lens of your goals. Sometimes a contact might offer you an opportunity that seems too good to pass up—until you realize that it doesn't fit in with your goals. You'll never get to your million dollar sales conversation if you keep getting sidetracked, and that is a very real possibility if you've put the maximum effort into building all of your relation-ships. After all, the better your relationships are, the more doors that will be opened to you. Having your goals written down will keep you on track and heading in the direction you want to go.

When writing down your goals, make sure that they're specific, measurable, achievable, relevant, and time-bound (SMART). Keep this acronym in mind when creating your goals and use it to help your contacts set their own goals. If you've created your own goals, helping others is a piece of cake. Helping your contacts figure out their goals is not only mentally rewarding but also can lead to a million dollar sales conversion because it helps you advance your relationships and discover where your goals overlap with theirs.

Step 3: Listen Actively

In order to help your customer meet his goals, you must be a great listener so that you can provide the best possible solution. But without a relationship, a positive attitude, and experience in setting your own goals, you may have trouble listening effectively to other people talk about their goals. Without being a truly good listener, you may miss what the other person's goal is entirely, whether it's because you just aren't goal-focused or you haven't taken the time to hone your listening skills. Then you won't be able to help them. If you do not listen effectively, you'll fail to develop relationships to the level they need to be before you will be able to find yourself in a million dollar sales conversation.

Don't be one of those people who smile and nod without really hearing what other people say. It's impossible to build relationships without listening actively. Instead, take note of the customer's body language and use it to decode what they're really saying.

Listen to their words—all of them—before you respond and then ask questions for clarification or just to learn more about who they are. Take what they say at face value without letting your own biases influence it. And perhaps the hardest part of all is: don't talk so much! Put the other person first and let them tell you their feelings and thoughts.

Take steps to remove some common barriers to effective listening, like environmental noise, distracting lighting, preconceived notions about the customer, or anything else that keeps you from actively listening to what the other person is saying.

Step 4: Be an Encourager

The more you listen carefully, the more you will realize that sometimes encouragement is appropriate. There are all sorts of ways you can encourage other people, but the basis for encouragement is this: treat someone as he should be (as author Steven Covey said).

It doesn't matter who you are encouraging. This same principle holds true, whether you're trying to encourage yourself, your sales team, or a customer. Studies show that staying positive and offering encouragement helps to reduce the length of sales slumps, so make encouragement a part of your daily routine. Listen to motivational tapes or read inspirational quotes. Do whatever you need to do to feel encouraged and then spread that encouragement around to others. They will see you as a very positive person with whom they want to have a relationship.

Remember: great things come from great relationships!

Step 5: Make Successful Small Talk for Continued Success

Encouragement leads to further exchange and a deepening relationship, and the further you take your relationship, the more you'll find the need to be able to make small talk. While it's true that you should make small talk in the beginning, this is something that grows along with the relationship.

When you first meet someone, it's important to make a good impression and not get straight to business. Ask questions about the other person to get them talking. Try to find something you have in common and build your relationship on that. Ask about the other person's life in a way that shows you care. This sets a solid foundation for a great long-term relationship.

As the relationship goes on, be sure to use your small talk abilities to check in with your contracts on a regular basis. Small talk should be a big part of your career because it is one of the key ingredients in million dollar sales conversations. When a customer is ready to sign a massive deal, they're going to remember the small talk you've had more than the business talks you've had. And why do you think this is? It's because small talk is the basis of relationships.

They will remember you as the person who always remembers the names of their kids and that their wife works at XYZ Company. They will remember that you're the one who sends them a birthday card every year. They'll remember that you were there at the funeral when their father died. They will remember the feeling of bonding and sharing they experienced the last time they did a deal with you, rather than the deal itself. And most of all, they will remember you because you've personalized the relationship and turned them into a friend and a partner.

Step 6: Stretch Your Network

Checking in with your contacts and making small talk from time to time is the best way to stay in touch and grow your network, expand it, and put it to work. The more you grow your relationships, the more new people you will find that you meet. Your contacts will want to introduce you to people they think you can help. They'll also want you to meet people they think can help you.

Your network should not be filled with people you never speak to. Be the one who takes 100 percent responsibility for the relationship and who makes regular contacts with people. Then put that network to work by expanding your network to meet people who know your contacts or who belong to the same groups and have similar goals. Become a thought leader people want to meet and network with, and you'll watch your network grow rapidly.

And then, when you start meeting more new people, start right back at the beginning of the cycle.

Get to Work!

All of this may seem like a lot to remember, but if you take the time to work on these things, soon they will become second-nature to you. So just pick one thing you feel needs the most work right now and focus on that, keeping the other things tucked away in the back of your mind.

Your own million dollar sales conversation is just around the corner. Start just one new relationship today and see where it takes you!

www.ingramcontent.com/pod-product-compliance
Lightning Source LLC
Chambersburg PA
CBHW060555200326
41521CB00007B/580